On Existentialism

On Existentialism

Mark Tanzer
University of Colorado at Denver

THOMSON
™
WADSWORTH

Australia • Brazil • Canada • Mexico • Singapore • Spain
United Kingdom • United States

On Existentialism
Mark Tanzer

Philosophy Editor: Worth Hawes
Series Editor: Robert Talisse
Assistant Editor: Patrick Stockstill
Editorial Assistant: Kamilah Lee
Technology Project Manager:
 Julie Aguilar
Marketing Manager: Christina Shea
Marketing Assistant: Mary Anne
 Payumo
Project Manager, Editorial Production:
 Marti Paul

Creative Director: Rob Hugel
Executive Art Director: Maria Epes
Print Buyer: Linda Hsu
Permissions Editor: Bob Kauser
Production Service/Compositor:
 Integra Software Services Pvt. Ltd.,
 Puducherry, India
Copy Editor: Sara Dovre Wudali
Cover and Text Printer:
 Thomson West

Printed in the United States of America
1 2 3 4 5 6 7 11 10 09 08 07

Library of Congress Control Number: 2007928694

ISBN-13: 978-0-495-00355-7
ISBN-10: 0-495-00355-7

Thomson Higher Education
10 Davis Drive
Belmont, CA 94002-3098
USA

For more information about our products, contact us at:
Thomson Learning Academic Resource Center
1-800-423-0563

For permission to use material from this text or product, submit a request online at **http://www.thomsonrights.com.** Any additional questions about permissions can be submitted by e-mail to **thomsonrights@thomson.com.**

For Victor

Acknowledgments

I would like to thank Robert Talisse for his patience during the completion of this book. I would also like to thank Ann Murphy for reading and commenting on an earlier version of the manuscript.

Contents

On Existentialism

Introduction

I. TOWARD A DEFINITION OF EXISTENTIALISM

Existentialism is a primarily European philosophical movement that flourished around the middle of the 20th century. Although existentialism is a 20th-century movement, the founders of existentialist philosophy were both 19th-century figures—Søren Kierkegaard (1813–1855) and Friedrich Nietzsche (1844–1900)—whose philosophical principles did not take root in mainstream academic philosophy until the 20th century.

Among philosophical movements, existentialism is somewhat unusual. For one thing, existentialism crossed the boundary between philosophy and literature to a greater extent than most philosophical movements did. Besides the existentialist philosophers, several novelists and playwrights are regularly characterized as existentialist, for example, Fyodor Dostoyevsky, Franz Kafka, Albert Camus, and Samuel Beckett. In addition, Jean-Paul Sartre (1905–1980), one of the most important existentialist philosophers, also wrote existentialist novels, short stories, and plays. Our concern, in this book, will focus on the existentialist philosophers.

Another peculiarity of existentialism is that few existentialist philosophers labeled themselves as such. In fact, Martin Heidegger (1889–1976), who is regarded as one of the giants of existentialist thought, explicitly eschewed the title. The main reason is that the existentialists rejected the idea of a philosophical system. That is, existentialist philosophers typically deny that the age-old philosophical ambition of articulating a rational systematic account of the world and the human beings inhabiting it is anything but a misguided project. Because of this aversion to systematic thought, existentialists maintain that no one definition can capture the essence of existentialist philosophy. To label a thinker as an *existentialist* presupposes that there is a final definition of existentialism by which that thinker's philosophy can be captured, but this conflicts with the anti-systematic claims of the existentialists. Nevertheless, an examination of existentialism demands that we couch that examination in a working definition thereof. This will give us at least a tentative foothold in the fundamental problematic that drove existentialist thought.

Although commentators have attempted to define existentialism in a variety of ways, a useful way to approach it is to focus on a basic *irrationalism* shared by existentialist thinkers. To understand this irrationalism, and thus to give ourselves a preliminary definition of existentialism, we must first understand the type of rationalism that existentialist irrationalism opposed. And the type of rationalism opposed by existentialism was first articulated by Plato—the first great systematic philosopher, whose form of rationalism has been a determining force of much of subsequent Western thought. But what, exactly, is Platonic rationalism?

II. PLATONIC RATIONALISM

The general nature of Platonic rationalism can be understood by way of Plato's famous distinction between knowledge and right opinion, which are two types of cognition. By *right opinion,* Plato refers to a vague, implicit grasp of what determines a thing to be the kind of thing that it is, whereas *knowledge* refers to a precise, explicit grasp thereof. For example, I have a certain cognitive grasp of how to get from my office to the room in which my morning class meets, that is, of what makes a certain route the route from my office to the classroom. Similarly, I have a cognitive grasp of how to walk up a flight of stairs, that is, of what makes a certain ordered set of bodily movements count as the bodily movements that constitute an instance of walking up the stairs. I can be sure that I have some cognitive grasp of both of these things because otherwise I would neither be able to make it to class nor to walk upstairs. But which of the two types of cognition that Plato distinguishes characterizes my grasp of these things? Do I have a precise, explicit grasp (i.e., knowledge) of the route to class and of the movements required to ascend stairs, or is my cognition thereof a vague, implicit grasp (i.e., right opinion)?

To answer these questions, consider what it would mean to have knowledge, in the Platonic sense, of the proper way to walk up a flight of stairs. In that case, I would possess a fully articulated account of, say, the angle at which I should bend my knee so I can place my foot on the next stair, as well as an explicit account of what percentage of my foot's surface area needs to be resting on the next stair to support my body as I begin to mount that stair, not to mention an explicit account of how much of my body weight would need to be shifted to the lead foot, and so on. If, on the other hand, I were to have right opinion, in the Platonic sense, of how to ascend stairs, then my cognition thereof would not have the precision and explicitness just described, but instead would be a vague, unarticulated sense of how to get up the stairs, an inexplicit grasp that allows me to walk up a flight of stairs but does not allow me to fully describe what, exactly, I do with my body when walking up a staircase. With regard to my cognition of the route from my office to the classroom, an analogous comparison between modes of cognition is easily constructed. Knowledge, in this case, would be the possession of a precise, fully articulated account of the route in question, including, say, how many classrooms I need to pass after entering the proper building, and other such details, whereas right opinion would be a vague sense that properly guides me to the classroom without allowing me to fully articulate the route thereto. In view of these descriptions, it is clear that in such cases our typical mode of cognition is right opinion rather than knowledge, and that the greater part of our cognition takes the form of right opinion. Most of our activities are based on right opinion, the cognition that allows us to recognize what makes something what it is without allowing us to say exactly what it is that we are thus recognizing.

Plato noticed how people had always allowed right opinion to guide their lives, and he maintained that there was a better way to live—on the basis of knowledge. A life guided by knowledge is, according to Plato, the examined life, and his discovery of the possibility of knowledge, along with the life guided thereby, instituted a revolution in Western thought, whose effects are still felt. To understand the nature of such a life, and its superiority over the life of right opinion, consider the following examples.

Suppose you are in a classroom that is several chairs short, and you are asked to get all of the chairs that might be in the hallway. In the hallway, you find three objects: a typical classroom chair, a bear trap, and a beanbag chair. How do you know which object to bring into the room? What sort of cognition would allow you to recognize which object is a chair? Right opinion is enough to allow you to recognize that the bear trap is not a chair; your vague implicit grasp of what makes a chair count as a chair allows you to immediately discount the bear trap from the class of chairs. Similarly, right opinion's vague sense of that which determines chairs as chairs suffices for designating the typical classroom chair as a chair. However, the case of the beanbag chair is, arguably, different.

On the one hand, the beanbag chair is chair-like enough to be called a beanbag *chair*, and so seems to possess the qualities that make a chair count as a chair. Still, it is also rather unchair-like. For if you did not know that such objects were called beanbag *chairs*, it is highly unlikely that you would designate them as chairs. Unlike the bear trap and the typical chair, it is not immediately obvious if the beanbag chair is a chair. It seems to be both chair-like and unchair-like at the same time. In other words, it is apparently ambiguous with regard to its being a chair or a non-chair. And the superiority of knowledge over right opinion comes to the fore with regard to such seemingly ambiguous objects.

Because of its apparent ambiguity, right opinion cannot definitively determine whether or not the beanbag chair is a chair; however, if you had *knowledge* of what makes a chair a chair, then you could make that determination. That is, with an explicit, fully articulated account of the qualities that make chairs belong to the class of chairs at your disposal, you could simply check to see if the object in question possesses those properties—if it has them, then it is, unquestionably, a chair; if it lacks any of them, then it is not. Thus, knowledge is superior to right opinion insofar as the latter mode of cognition does not allow us to definitively determine the conceptual identity of apparently ambiguous objects. We can only make a relatively informed guess about whether such objects belong to a given class, and such guesses can turn out to be wrong. Simply put, knowledge takes the guesswork out of such judgments by arming us with an explicit, definitive criterion by which to carry out such judgments.

At this point, it could be argued that a life based on knowledge may allow us to effectively classify objects such as chairs, but that the ability to properly classify objects does not seem to result in a superior form of life. After all, if I, say, mistakenly classify beanbag chairs as chairs, it is not as though this will result in a significantly deficient life. Mistaking bear traps for chairs would reduce the quality of my life, but right opinion is sufficient for avoiding that mistake. Thus, precious little seems to hang on the move from a life of right opinion to one of knowledge. But if we apply the principles discussed thus far to more important conceptual decisions, then the significance of this Platonic distinction becomes clear and compelling. This can be seen by way of the following examples.

Suppose I were to base my ethical decisions on mere right opinion. In many cases, this vague, implicit sense of what makes a course of action count as good or evil would be enough to guide me through an ethically good life, thereby making me a good person. For instance, if I see someone desperately scrambling to get out of the path of an oncoming bus, it would obviously be good to help that person to safety and just as obviously evil to actively prevent the person from avoiding the bus. Here, my right opinion with regard to what makes a good action good allows me to classify, and properly choose between, the possible courses of action, just as my right opinion regarding the properties that make chairs count as chairs allowed me to recognize that the typical chair was a chair and that the bear trap was not. But right opinion about the ethical classification of actions can fail us when we face courses of action whose ethical quality is apparently ambiguous, just as it failed us when faced with objects of seemingly questionable conceptual identity, such as the beanbag chair.

Courses of action that appear to be ethically ambiguous might include euthanizing a suffering family member. Just as the beanbag chair seemed to be both chair-like and unchair-like, so euthanasia seems to be both good and evil. For just as it was unclear if the beanbag chair possessed the qualities that make a chair a chair, it is unclear if euthanasia possesses the qualities that determine an ethically good action as such. After all, it seems that ending suffering is good, but it also seems that ending a life is not.

In such cases, right opinion abandons us to guessing which course of action to pursue, and here the fallibility of right opinion is a serious matter. Whereas a wrong guess about the conceptual identity of a beanbag chair does not carry serious consequences, a wrong guess regarding the ethical quality of euthanasia does because, in this case, one's own ethical character is at stake. Hence, the importance of a life guided by knowledge. For just as an explicit, fully articulated account of the qualities that make chairs chairs allows us to definitively determine whether an apparently ambiguous object is, in fact, a chair, so such an account of what makes good actions good allows definitive determinations of morally proper courses of action. Knowledge, then, takes the guesswork out of our attempt to lead an ethically good life; it opens up the possibility of being infallible in our ethical judgments.

In view of the previous discussion, we can see why so much of Plato's writings are occupied with attempts to define various terms. The search for explicit accounts of the properties that make things the types of things that they are is the search for definitions. And the completion of this search, by which right opinion is converted into knowledge, is tantamount to the attainment of a superior—examined—life. For Plato, this conversion, in which what is implicitly cognized is made explicit, *is* philosophy.

Thus far, our sketch of Platonic rationalism has focused on issues concerning our cognition of things—epistemological issues. To conclude this preliminary account, we must now note the particular conception of the objects of cognition that is presupposed by Plato's distinction between right opinion and knowledge. In more technical terms, we must take notice of how Plato's *epistemological* position is grounded in a particular *ontological* position, that is, a theory of what it is for a thing to be a thing.

As we have seen, Plato's basic epistemological claim is that things can be explicitly known. That is, the conceptual identity of any thing can be articulated in a determinate, unambiguous formula; in this way, human knowledge can fully understand the world. And for that to be possible, the world must be composed of objects with determinate, unambiguous natures that make them what they are. Thus, although the conceptual identity of a thing may seem to be ambiguous, as in the case of the beanbag chair, the ambiguity is merely apparent. The illusory appearance of indeterminacy in things disappears through the philosophical conversion of right opinion to knowledge.

Hence, Platonism is a form of *rationalism* because it holds that the world is, ultimately, rational in the sense that it is structured by unambiguous, determinate principles. These principles, which Plato calls "Forms," are the formulas that give things their determinate conceptual identities. And the philosophical project of attaining knowledge is the attempt to articulate these determinate structuring principles, thereby yielding a full understanding of the world. It is the rational mind's attempt to grasp the rational structure of the world; it

is the proper exercise of the distinguishing characteristic of humanity—
its possession of reason.

III. EXISTENTIALIST IRRATIONALISM

We can now get an initial sense of the irrationalism that lies at the
heart of existentialist philosophy. In opposition to the Platonist claim
that things in the world are what they are in accordance with rational,
unambiguous principles, that the world is rational, and thus that
ambiguities in the world are merely apparent; the existentialist claims
that things *really are* ambiguous, that there are no unambiguous
principles constituting that world—the world, for the existentialist,
is irrational. Although the Platonist maintains that things have univocal conceptual identities, rendering things conceptually determinate, and thus that conceptual indeterminacies are mere appearances;
the existentialist maintains that things really are conceptually indeterminate. For the Platonist, to be is to be determinate; for the existentialist, to be is to be indeterminate.

Given the existentialist's denial of the world's rationality, the
Platonist's epistemological aspiration of converting right opinion to
knowledge, and thus attaining an explicit, articulable grasp of the
world's structure, is seen by the existentialist as, in principle, impossible. For the world, being irrational, cannot be fully grasped through
the determinate formulas of rational thought. Instead, a proper understanding of the world occurs through a mode of cognition that works
with the ambiguities inherent in the world, whether these ambiguities
pertain to the conceptual identities of things, the ethical qualities of
actions, or to any other aspects of that which is. Existentialism
endorses modes of cognition that consider the indeterminacy of the
world, rather than modes, such as Platonic knowledge, that endorse
the false ideal of overcoming the world's indeterminacy.

Thus, we can easily see why existentialism is commonly regarded
as a pessimistic, destructive philosophy. Existentialism attacks the
ground of many of modern Western culture's most cherished beliefs.
Its rejection of the world's rationality, and thus of rational thought's
ability to fully understand the world, undermines such basic Western
institutions as science and morality. This negative aspect of existentialism will be explored in the following chapters. However, existentialism is not a purely negative philosophy. The existentialists have

also endeavored to explicate the primary characteristics of the world's irrationality, as well as ways to respond to this irrationality. Thus, existentialist philosophy is both a denial of a traditional way of understanding the world and humanity's place in it, and an attempt to articulate a new way of understanding the world and our place therein. The latter constitutes the positive aspect of existentialism, which will also be explored in this book.

Although our characterization of existentialism as fundamentally a form of irrationalism is certainly not the only legitimate characterization thereof, there are distinct advantages that follow from using this characterization as the foundation for our study. To see these advantages, we first consider the purpose of a supplemental study, such as ours, that introduces a philosophical movement, be it existentialism or any other such movement. Simply put, a supplemental study should facilitate the reading and the understanding of primary sources. But the question to be asked concerns the best way of providing such facilitation, and we can distinguish two opposed ways of answering this question.

On the one hand, a supplemental study could present a detailed account of a selection of an author's writings. In this way, the reader becomes acquainted with specific works—with the problems there addressed by the author, the meanings of technical terms used, and so forth. On the other hand, a supplemental study could articulate the general structural principles underlying an author's thought. Here, the details of the author's writings are seen as expressions of the underlying principles guiding that author's thought. And it is with these general principles, rather than their particular manifestations, that the reader of such a study becomes acquainted.

The first approach has its advantages. Sections of commentary are readily correlated with sections of original text, guiding the reader through the selected works of the author under consideration. The reader emerges conversant with the details of the primary sources treated. However, this approach also has its disadvantages. First, because of its focus on the specific details of specific works, such a commentary has diminished, if any, applicability to writings beyond those commented upon. It directly facilitates the understanding of only a limited number of primary sources. In addition, this approach tends to yield a fairly disunified picture both of the authors whose works are treated and, more importantly, of the philosophical movement that they exemplify. Specific details of an author's works are exhibited, but not the underlying principles that such details manifest and that lend unity to them. The resulting disunity also leaves the reader without a unified conception of the philosophical movement examined by a supplemental study that takes this approach. Without general principles to unify the works of the authors belonging to a philosophical movement, there are no such principles to unify the movement itself.

These inadequacies are remedied by the second approach to writing a supplemental study, that is, focusing on general underlying principles rather than on textual details. This approach abstracts out the general, formal principles from which the particular, concrete details of an author's work are derived. In this way, the reader is provided with a structural, formal lens through which all of the works of a given author can be read. Rather than leading the reader through the myriad details of a selected set of writings, the reader is given the structural principles from which the entirety of an author's writings can be understood. Moreover, the highlighting of general principles yields a unified picture of the writings of a given author, as well as of the philosophical movement exemplified therein.

Of course, the second approach has disadvantages. The reader acquires fewer of the details, and less of the technical terminology, of the writings of the authors considered. More importantly, the focus on generalities runs the risk of giving an over-simplified picture of an author or philosophical movement. Subtleties may be glossed over in the move to general principles. But for the purposes of a supplemental study, the disadvantages of the second approach constitute the lesser of two evils. To gain an understanding of a philosophical movement, the first order of business is the acquisition of a general account thereof. Subtleties and nuances come later, and will only muddy the waters at this preliminary stage. For this reason, our study introduces the reader to existentialist philosophy through an examination of what I take to be its most basic principle, that is, the fundamentally indeterminate, and thus irrational, nature of all existence—the world's lack of unambiguous structuring principles.

The problematic character of the first approach is particularly dangerous when applied to a supplemental study of, specifically, existentialism. One of the hallmarks of existentialist thought is its denigration of abstract structural principles. That is, the existentialist revolt against Platonic rationalism includes a valorization of individual, concrete phenomena, in contrast with the Platonic tradition's valorization of general, abstract principles. The precise reasons that the existentialist rejection of Platonic rationalism takes this form will be seen later, in the section on Kierkegaard's ontology. Still, we can already see how this tenet of existentialism tends to skew supplemental studies toward the first approach outlined above.

The existentialist's turn away from abstract principles is often taken to imply that there are no such principles proper to existentialist thought. If this were actually the case, then the only accurate way to explain existentialist thought would be to recount the descriptions of concrete life found in the works of existentialist authors, along with the technical terminology used in these descriptions. And, in fact, existentialist authors dedicate a great deal of their writings to the explication of such concrete details. Hence, the apparent propriety of focusing a supplemental study on these details, and this is the approach that such studies typically take. The result, however, is usually a welter of statements about the complexity of everyday life, about the difficulties intrinsic to concrete human existence, along with loosely connected discussions of the vast array of technical terms employed by existentialist authors to describe these phenomena. In this way, the reader is given the impression that the disunity suffered by supplemental studies that take this approach is inherent in existentialist thought itself. Existentialism seems to be composed of a loosely connected group of writers, without any principles to tie them together. Moreover, this characterization promotes a stereotypical view of existentialism that has cast suspicion on its properly philosophical character, on the extent to which existentialist philosophy is really a philosophy at all. The stereotypical view is that existentialist authors eschew the entire apparatus of traditional philosophical analysis, by refusing to ground their claims about the nature of the world and of the human being in underlying principles. Instead, existentialists are seen as promulgating their own peculiar, idiosyncratic views of the world, which are based on their parochial observations of the human condition—views that are then presented to their readers through a fog of obscure technical terminology.

By grounding existentialist thought in the basic principle of the indeterminacy of all that exists, and by deriving from this principle the specific doctrines regarding the nature of the world and of the human being held by existentialist philosophers, we hope to give a unified picture of the existentialist movement, and to take a step toward overcoming the stereotypical view of existentialism. In the interest of doctrinal unity, our examination of the details of specific works will be kept to a minimum. That is, such details will be examined only insofar as they exhibit the general principle of the indeterminacy of existence. The same goes for the extent to which technical terminology will be introduced and explained. Readers should then be equipped to independently pursue further study of existentialist writings, and to decipher the technical terminology contained therein. And in the interest of overcoming the stereotypical view of existentialism, our analysis will attempt to show not only that existentialist thought is grounded in the underlying principle of the indeterminacy of all that exists, but that this principle is arrived at through the traditional methods of philosophical argumentation. The intended result is a picture of existentialism that may be somewhat unusual, but that gives this form of thought a properly philosophical viability. Moreover, our study intends to give the reader a way of attaining at least a preliminary foothold in the variety of texts customarily grouped together as existentialist.

Our study will be divided as follows. We will begin with the existentialist conception of the basic structure of the world itself, or existentialist ontology. We will then investigate how the existentialist worldview affects our conception of the way that we ought to behave in such a world, our conception of good and evil, or existentialist ethics. Both discussions will examine the thought of four paradigmatic figures in the existentialist tradition: Nietzsche, Kierkegaard, Heidegger, and Sartre.

1

Ontology

I. NIETZSCHE'S ONTOLOGY—THE WORLD
AS WILL TO POWER

As we have seen, existentialist ontology maintains that the world is irrational in the sense that it is not structured by determinate, unambiguous principles. But what, exactly, would the character of such a world be? How can we get a foothold in the idea of an ambiguous, indeterminate world? Are there any familiar, everyday phenomena that we can use as clear manifestations of the world's ambiguity? We have already broached the topic of ambiguous, indeterminate objects in our consideration of the beanbag chair as apparently straddling the conceptual line between chairs and non-chairs. Could beanbag chairs, then, serve as our paradigm example of an indeterminate object from which we could, in turn, derive the structure of the existentialist's world of ontological indeterminacy? Unfortunately not, because, as we have seen, the Platonist can easily blame such apparent ambiguities on the unsophisticated mode of cognition with which we approach them—mere opinion. According to the Platonist, once we fulfill our mission, as rational beings, of attaining knowledge, of understanding the true structure of the world, we will discover that such objects simply are what they are—unambiguously. This thing in front of me either is, in fact, a chair or it is not, regardless of my ability or inability to recognize which is the case.

Our search for a way into existentialist ontology, then, must begin with something whose ambiguity could not be reduced to mere appearance. Are there such irreducibly ambiguous phenomena?

Friedrich Nietzsche believed that the *will* was an example thereof, and so he based his ontology of "will to power" on the nature of will. To understand Nietzsche's notion of will to power, which he takes to be the fundamental structure of all existence, it is helpful to first take a brief detour into the thought of the ancient Greek philosopher Heraclitus. Heraclitus, who predated Plato by approximately 70 years, was a strong influence on Nietzsche; in Heraclitus's ontology, Nietzsche saw an articulation of a fundamentally indeterminate world. The phenomenon on which Heraclitus based his ontology was change. And, as we will see, Nietzsche's ontology of will displays essential similarities with Heraclitus' ontology of change.

According to Heraclitus, the world is fundamentally a world of constant change, and so an analysis of the basic structure of change will yield an account of the basic structure of the world. Heraclitus finds change to be structured as a unity of opposites. This follows from the fact that change is a transition from something (call it A) being the case to something different (not-A) being the case. And so, that which undergoes change cannot itself be any more A than it is not-A, or else it would not be *a* thing that changes. For if it were, say, A rather than not-A, then it could not change into not-A without losing its identity, and thus simply disappearing only to be replaced by not-A, rather than changing into not-A. Alternatively, if it were not-A rather than A, then it could never have been A in the first place, and so could not have changed from A into not-A. In other words, that which undergoes change must be just as much A as it is not-A. In this sense, it is both A and not-A; it unifies opposites.

Given that Heraclitus sees the world as characterized primarily by its ever-changing nature, and that the structure of that which changes is to be and not be what it is, the fundamental structure of the world is ambiguous, indeterminate. This ambiguous world-structuring principle is what Heraclitus calls the *logos*. Nietzsche finds the same fundamental ambiguity in the structure of will that Heraclitus finds in the structure of change. Thus, he believes that the world's indeterminacy can be understood by conceiving the world as a world of will. To see why Nietzsche thinks of the will as indeterminately structured, we must see what, exactly, his notion of will amounts to.

For Nietzsche, the nature of will is most clearly manifested in the phenomenon of desire. More specifically, will is manifested in desire insofar as desire is always a movement beyond itself, and insofar as desire is unfulfillable, beyond any possible satisfaction. And although desires can be, and often are, fulfilled, Nietzsche's position is that if we focus on a certain aspect of desire, the structure of the world's ambiguity will become visible. What Nietzsche wants us to use, to gain a foothold in the idea of an ambiguous world, is the notion of desire taken purely in its striving aspect, desire as pure striving—in abstraction from its fulfillment. This may be a mere abstraction, but Nietzsche only uses it to illustrate the structure of ontological indeterminacy, not to claim that he has discovered that all desires are in fact unfulfillable.

Desire, thought as pure striving, is unfulfillable. For when desire is fulfilled, it stops striving; desire only strives as long as it is unsatisfied. Therefore, to conceive desire in terms of its dimension of striving alone is to conceive it as unfulfillable. And it is also to conceive desire as always moving beyond itself. For as long as desire is unfulfilled, it strives toward fulfillment, toward changing from the state that it is currently in to a different state that is closer to satisfaction. That is, unfulfilled desire never rests; it continually transcends the state that it is in. And in doing so, it is constantly becoming different than what it is at any given moment. Therefore, to conceive desire in terms of its dimension of striving alone is to conceive it as moving beyond itself, as transcending itself.

So, desire as pure striving is an unfulfillable movement beyond itself. And this, for Nietzsche, is the fundamental structure of an ambiguous, indeterminate world—the fundamental structure of the world as will. But how is this unfulfillable self-transcending movement ambiguous? Recall that the existentialist's assertion of the world's ambiguity is the claim that things in the world have no determinate, univocal conceptual identity. And Nietzsche's version of this claim says that all that exists is will. Our current question concerning the ambiguity of Nietzschean will, then, asks, How does unfulfillable self-transcendence lack a univocal conceptual identity?

To answer this question, we begin by distinguishing the idea of a thing whose self-transcendence is fulfillable from a thing whose self-transcendence is not. In the former case, the thing under consideration is beset by a kind of instability. As self-transcendent, it continually moves beyond the state that it is in, becoming different than what it was at any previous moment. This instability may seem to be tantamount to the conceptual ambiguity characteristic of existentialist ontology because a thing that continually transcends itself apparently lacks a stable self, and thus a determinate identity. Always becoming different, such a thing cannot be univocally identified with any of the particular states that it embodies throughout its self-transcending career. If it were to be so identified, then it could not transcend itself.

That is, it could not be *a* self-transcending thing for the same reasons that, for Heraclitus, *a* changing thing could not be identified with its pre-change nor its post-change embodiments. The instability of the self-transcendent, then, seems to imply its ontological ambiguity. However, this is not necessarily the case; a closer look at the structure of self-transcendence will show that *fulfillable* self-transcendent things do possess a univocal conceptual identity.

Although a self-transcendent thing's identity is unstable in view of the ever-changing states of itself that it embodies, its identity is stabilized if its self-transcendence aims at a fulfillment of that self-transcending movement, a state of rest toward which its continual mutations are directed. For, in that case, its various states, the alterations between which it is driven by its pursuit of a state of fulfillment, are unified by their relation to that overarching aim. That is, although each state of the self-transcendent thing is different, they are different states of the same thing insofar as each state is the state that it is, has its very identity defined, by virtue of its relation to the ultimate aim of those differing states. We can clarify this with an example.

Suppose I am climbing an eight-runged ladder, and that my goal is to reach the top rung. Suppose further that the only characteristics I possess are my positions on the ladder; in other words, we are considering my identity strictly with regard to my being the climber of the ladder. At each moment, a description of the state that I am in, and thus of myself, will be different. For instance, the following progression could occur: at time T1, I am at the foot of the ladder; at T2, I am on the second rung of the ladder; at T3, I am on the fourth rung of the ladder; and at T4, I am on the second rung (but, unlike at T2, I am on the right side of the rung). The question here is this: Given that my identity is always determined exclusively by my place on the ladder, that is, given that we are considering me exclusively as climber of this ladder, and given that my place on the ladder is, at each moment, different than it was at the previous moment, what allows me to maintain my identity throughout these changes? On what grounds could it be said that I am *a* ladder climber? Why are the four temporal moments enumerated not descriptions of four different things appearing at four different locations on the ladder at four different times?

As I negotiate the ladder, my identity can be maintained, even though I am different at each moment, only if the various states that I embody are defined in terms of their proximity to the goal of these states—only if my self-transcendence aims at a fulfillment. This can be seen through the following considerations.

Notice that when we define my various states without regard to their proximity to a fulfillment, as we did earlier, the relations between those states are purely external. That is, the states of being at the locations designated as "at the foot of the ladder," "on the second rung," and "on the fourth rung," have no internal relation to one another; each is articulated in a formula that refers to the location itself and nothing beyond it. This fact, and the significance thereof, can be seen more clearly by noting another way of defining these various states, specifically, a way of defining them in terms of their proximity to a fulfillment.

We can redefine my various states as I climb the ladder as follows: at T1, I am eight rungs from reaching the top rung; at T2, I am six rungs from reaching the top rung; at T3, I am four rungs from reaching the top rung; and at T4, I am six rungs from reaching the top rung (but, unlike at T2, I am on the right side of the rung). These descriptions exhibit internal relations to each other through their common reference to the ladder's top rung. This common reference unifies my various states in that my being at those locations on the ladder is conceived not simply as the occupations of different spatial locations, but as approximations to their fulfillment, that is, as moments of growth or decay. And for various states to count as states of growth or decay, they must be states of *one* thing. Therefore, even though, as I climb the ladder, I am different at each moment insofar as the states that I embody are continually different, that these varying states have an aim whose occurrence would fulfill, and thus bring to rest, the alteration of states, the varying embodiments are of *a* thing— their having an aim forges a univocal identity for the self-transcendent thing that I am as I climb the ladder.

The upshot of the foregoing analysis is that a self-transcendent thing is not conceptually ambiguous as long as its self-transcending movement admits of an ultimate fulfillment. Notice that such fulfill-ment need not ever actually occur in order for the goal of fulfillment can play its role as the source of conceptual identity. Having an aim determines the varying states as instances of growth and decay, whether or not that aim is ever met. Thus, even if I were never to reach the top rung of the ladder, my various states could still be described as internally related, as long as they all aim at reaching the top rung. In fact, achievement of such an aim need not even be possible for it to play its identity-determining role. To illustrate this, suppose that my goal in climbing the ladder is not simply to reach the top rung, but to reach the top rung so that I can use it as a platform from which to jump onto the surface of the sun. Although my goal of landing on the sun is actually impossible, it can still unify my ladder-climbing states. Even such an unreachable goal can be approximated, and so can forge the internal relatedness of states required to unify them as moments of growth or decay, and therefore as various states of one thing. All that is required is that the idea of fulfillment set a standard by which the self-transcendent thing's states can be judged as better or worse approximations with regard to that standard.

Here, it should be noted that such a standard would not be provided by an impossible fulfillment if that fulfillment were impossible because it is self-contradictory, or logically impossible, rather than being merely physically impossible. For instance, suppose that my goal as I climb the ladder is, ultimately, to turn into a four-sided triangle. Such an object, being self-contradictory, is really nothing at all, and so my various states cannot be better or worse approximations with regard to it. They cannot, then, be instances of growth or decay, and so they cannot be differing states of the same thing.

The previous discussion has revealed the structure of fulfillable, or fulfillment-driven, self-transcendence. More precisely, we have sketched the structure of a self-transcendent thing that aims at a fulfillment that is at least logically possible, a self-transcendent thing that is fulfillable in the sense that its fulfillment is possible *in principle*. And we have found that, because of this fulfillability, such things are not conceptually ambiguous. With this in mind, Nietzsche's existentialist picture of the world begins to take shape.

As we have seen, Nietzsche's world of will is ambiguous insofar as its basic structure is that of unfulfillable self-transcendence. We can now see why a self-transcendent thing must be unfulfillable to be ambiguous—relation to a logically possible goal lends a univocal conceptual identity to a self-transcendent thing. However, it does not seem that the actually existing world really is ambiguous in the Nietzschean sense. After all, even if we accept, with Nietzsche, that the world is constantly changing, that the world is self-transcendent, it seems to be more like a fulfillable self-transcendent thing than an unfulfillable one, and so Nietzsche seems to be offering a highly distorted picture of the world. To better understand this criticism, we must take a closer look at our previous descriptions of fulfillable and unfulfillable self-transcendence.

Recall that we drew the distinction between fulfillable and unfulfillable self-transcendence by conceiving of myself as the climber of an eight-runged ladder, and then noting the effects on my possession of a conceptual identity that followed from conceiving of my positions on the ladder as either having or lacking an ultimate goal. This yielded two conceptions of myself as climber of the ladder, from which two ways of viewing the world can be derived by analogy. Analogous to my ladder-climbing states as having a goal, in which case I, as ladder-climber, possess a univocal conceptual identity, is a world whose various states aim at a goal, a world possessing the structure of fulfillable self-transcendence. Such a world would be one whose states are internally related, and therefore a world in which objects maintain their identities across time.

But what sort of world would be analogous to the situation in which my various states on the ladder lack any reference to a goal, a world of unfulfillable self-transcendence? Without any unifying aim, my ladder-climbing states had no internal relations to each other, so I lacked a conceptual identity; my ladder-climbing states were completely disconnected. Analogous to my ladder-climbing states conceived as lacking a goal, then, is a world whose various states have no reference to a goal, and thus a world whose states are completely disconnected. Objects in such a world would not maintain their identities across time; it would be a world in which objects do not endure, but instead are replaced by completely new objects as soon as they come into existence. Things would inexplicably appear out of nowhere and would just as inexplicably be extinguished, only to be replaced by different, immediately extinguished objects.

To conceive the world as fulfillable self-transcendence, then, is to conceive a world in which objects endure, whereas objects in a world conceived as unfulfillable self-transcendence do not. And, surely, objects in the world actually do have some degree of endurance. Although things may move beyond themselves, taking on ever-new states, they are still enduring, stable things, and the world is one unified world. Hence, the apparent implausibility of Nietzsche's existentialist view of the world as irrational in the sense of possessing the structure of unfulfillable self-transcendence.

To defend Nietzsche against this criticism, we must note that unfulfillable self-transcendent things need not be conceived as popping in and out of existence in the manner described earlier. An alternative view of unfulfillable self-transcendence can be glimpsed in Heraclitus's ontology of change, which, as we have seen, was highly influential on Nietzsche's thought. Rather than conceiving of ambiguous, unfulfillable self-transcendent things as manifested in atomistic, unrelated states, and thus as failing to be enduring *things* at all,

Heraclitus conceives such things as flowing from one state to another. Such a view of self-transcendence has the advantage of giving a more accurate description of the world as we experience it; we do experience things as flowing from one state to another, and thereby maintaining at least a momentary stability across time. The problem, from a Nietzschean point of view, is how to understand such identity without having to posit an ultimate fulfillment unifying the various states of the self-transcendent thing, and thereby falling into the Platonic rationalism that Nietzsche's existentialist ontology repudiates. In other words, the question becomes: how can self-transcendent things maintain even a temporary identity without being fulfillable, without possessing a univocal conceptual identity?

A self-transcendent thing can exhibit self-identity, and thus can endure, even without being fulfillable, if it is conceived neither as simply lacking a goal nor as aiming at a determinate goal, but instead as having an *indeterminate*, or ambiguous goal. This can be understood by considering the following. As we have seen, a self-transcendent thing with a determinate goal is fulfillable, such as myself as ladder-climber with the goal of reaching the top rung of the ladder that I am climbing. Let us represent such a fulfillable self-transcendent thing as S, and its reaching its goal as its being G. As S approaches G, it becomes more G-like; in our example, as I get closer to the top rung, my state becomes more like being on the top rung. In other words, states in which a fulfillable self-transcendent thing exhibits growth are states by which it becomes more G-like; alternatively, states in which such a thing exhibits decay are states by which it becomes less G-like. And the fulfillable self-transcendent thing maintains an enduring identity by virtue of its states being thus conceivable as states of growth or decay.

We have also seen that a self-transcendent thing with no goal at all is unfulfillable, as when we considered my ladder-climbing states without reference to a goal. Having no goal, such a thing cannot exhibit growth or decay, and so it does not maintain an enduring identity. And, as we have seen, neither of these serves as a viable model for Nietzsche's conception of the world as unfulfillable self-transcendence, of the world as will. But we have overlooked a third possibility.

Suppose that my ladder-climbing states did not aim at a determinate goal but, rather than simply lacking a goal, had an indeterminate goal. Let us represent such a self-transcendent thing as S_i; and, because its goal is ambiguous, let us represent its reaching its goal as its being G/not-G. Like the fulfillable self-transcendent thing, S_i's various states can be seen as states of growth or decay. For instance, a change in S_i's state might amount to its being more G-like, and so could be characterized as exhibiting growth insofar as its goal possesses a G-like dimension. However, because S_i's goal also possesses a non-G-like dimension, that is, because S_i's goal is ambiguous, a change by which S_i becomes more non-G-like could also be characterized as exhibiting growth. Either of these changes could also be characterized as instances of decay, depending on which aspect of S_i's ambiguous goal is focused on. Therefore, a self-transcendent thing with an indeterminate, ambiguous goal exhibits growth and decay, and so such a thing possesses an enduring identity.

But S_i is distinguished from the fulfillable self-transcendent thing, which also possesses an enduring identity, insofar as S_i's goal is in principle unattainable because of its indeterminate character. For instance, if we were to take changes by which S_i becomes more G-like as instances of growth, such growth could never be fulfilled because S_i's goal has both a G dimension and a non-G dimension, and so if S_i were to become completely G-like, it would lose the non-G dimension that is intrinsic to its fulfillment. Thus, a self-transcendent thing with an indeterminate goal has an identity insofar as it has a goal, but the indeterminacy of that goal renders the attainment thereof impossible in principle.

The indeterminacy of S_i's goal also renders S_i's own identity indeterminate. This can be seen by noting the specific way in which S_i's identity is characterized in relation to its identity-determining goal, as opposed to the way that a fulfillable self-transcendent thing's identity is so characterized. In the latter case, S's identity is determined, throughout its changing states, by its being more or less G-like. Each of S's states, and thus S's identity, can be unambiguously characterized because of G's unambiguous nature. That is, the univocal nature of S's goal renders S's identity univocal. Similarly, S_i's identity is determined, throughout its changing states, by its relation to its goal—in this case, by its relation to G/not-G. But S_i's states cannot be univocally characterized because its goal is ambiguous. For instance, a state that renders S_i more G-like is a state by which it can be characterized as closer to its goal (insofar as S_i's goal has a G dimension) and at the same time further from its goal (insofar as S_i's goal has a non-G dimension). Thus, a self-transcendent thing with an indeterminate goal maintains an identity across time, but its identity is as indeterminate as is its identity-determining goal.

The previous conception of a self-transcendent thing with an indeterminate goal best captures Nietzsche's conception of the world as will. According to Nietzsche's existentialist ontology, his ontology of the world's fundamental indeterminacy, the basic structure of the world is that of will in the sense of desire as pure striving. And the structure of desire as pure striving is that of unfulfillable self-transcendence in the sense of that which continually transforms itself in view of an ambiguous goal. The world as will, then, is in a state of constant flux, though maintaining an ambiguous identity—it is pure ambiguity, pure indeterminacy. This structural indeterminacy renders things in the world fundamentally ambiguous. The ever-changing things in the world are not univocally this type of thing or that type of thing, but are, so to speak, gray areas. Ultimately, we could say that for Nietzsche all existence, being will, is pure gray area. It is a world of ambiguous, mutating things, flowing ceaselessly toward nothing determinable, nothing that could be attained.

One final issue to be addressed regarding Nietzsche's conception of the world as will concerns the connection between will and power. Why does Nietzsche characterize will as will *to power?* For Nietzsche, will, and thus all existence, is will to power insofar as will, understood in the sense articulated earlier, pursues its own growth. That is, as self-transcendent, will constantly transforms itself, becoming different than it was; will always overcomes itself, and in this sense continually grows, becomes more. This is the nature of Nietzschean power—to be powerful is to be self-transforming, self-overcoming, rather than confined by a determinate, unyielding identity. But because Nietzschean will has no determinate, attainable goal, its growth does not aim at some final state. Instead, will simply grows; it grows for the sake of its own growth. Will, then, is will toward growth, and, given Nietzsche's identification of growth with power, will is will to power.

With this conception of the Nietzschean world in mind, we can now understand some of the various ways that Nietzsche characterizes the world. Explicating these characterizations will also give us a clearer picture of the Nietzschean world. We begin with Nietzsche's most famous claim—that "God is dead." The first question to be answered regarding this Nietzschean doctrine is this: Who or what is this "God" that Nietzsche claims to be dead? We approach this question by examining some examples of what Nietzsche calls "shadows of God," which are the various ways of interpreting the world that are rooted in the belief in God. From these manifestations of the belief in God, we will be able to infer what, exactly, those who believe in God believe in.

At this point, it may seem that an inquiry into the nature of Nietzsche's conception of God is unnecessary. It is well-known that Nietzsche was an outspoken critic of Christianity, so it stands to reason that his proclamation of God's death is a proclamation of the untenability of Christianity, as well as of any religion that affirms the existence of an all-powerful supernatural being, or anything of the sort. However, Nietzsche uses the term *God* to refer to a much broader category of phenomena than simply the God posited by various religions, although the religious God falls within this category. That Nietzsche's deceased God is not simply the God of religion, and therefore that those who believe in God are not simply religious people, is confirmed by noting a couple of the examples of God's shadows that Nietzsche cites. These divine shadows are the interpretation of the world that views it as though it were an organism and the interpretation of the world that views it as though it were a machine, or the teleological and mechanistic worldviews, respectively.

The teleological worldview attempts to understand the world by drawing an analogy between the world and an organism. Specifically, it maintains that occurrences in the world, like the activities of an organism, are driven by the pursuit of a goal, a final, ideal state-of-affairs toward which the world strives. This worldview, which is typical of pre-scientific Western thought, sees the driving force behind worldly events as lying in a future state that the world pursues and so is yet to be actualized. For example, teleologists might say that the world pursues a state in which its inhabitants are happy. With this in mind, they might say that it is now raining because rain will help this year's crops to grow, which is conducive to the happiness of the world's inhabitants. The growth of this year's crops and, ultimately, the happiness of living things, although these things have not yet occurred, are seen as causing the rain. They exert their causal power insofar as they are states-of-affairs that the world pursues.

With the birth of modern science, the teleological worldview was replaced by the mechanistic worldview, which conceives of the world as analogous to a machine. Specifically, the mechanistic worldview maintains that occurrences in the world, like the functioning of a machine, are set in motion by previous occurrences. For example, mechanists might say that it is now raining because of certain chemical reactions that have taken place in the clouds, which in turn cause other meteorological occurrences, ultimately resulting in rain. For the mechanist, then, the driving force behind worldly events lies not in a future state that is yet to be actualized but, rather, in past events.

In view of these examples of God's shadows, of worldviews that are rooted in a belief in God, in the Nietzschean sense, it is clear that believing in God and being religious are far from equivalent. It is possible to be an atheist while holding a teleological or mechanistic worldview. So, what, exactly, is it that leads Nietzsche to classify these worldviews together, as shadows of God, despite their clear differences? Both maintain that the world is structured by unambiguous, determinate principles. In other words, both are forms of the Platonic rationalism that Nietzsche's existentialist ontology opposes. The rationalist roots of the teleological and mechanistic pictures can be seen through the following considerations.

In the case of the teleological worldview, the principle that structures the world is the ultimate goal at which all worldly events aim. This principle is unambiguous in that it is a determinate, fully articulable state-of-affairs. And it gives structure to worldly events insofar as such events are what they are in relation to it; events are defined by their degree of approximation thereto. In the terminology that we used earlier, the teleologist sees the world as fulfillable self-transcendence, with the world's ultimate goal serving as that which gives the world's various states their univocal conceptual identity. The teleological worldview, then, asserts an unambiguous, rational world.

In the case of the mechanistic worldview, each event is what it is insofar as it is part of the chain of causes and effects that constitute the functioning of the world-machine. An event's identity is determined by its place within this causal chain. The principles that structure the world, then, are the laws that determine how the causal chain functions, that determine which events cause and are caused by which other events—the scientific laws of nature. The mechanist sees these laws as unambiguous, formulable rules, such as the law of gravity. Thus, the mechanist, like the teleologist, claims that the world is rational.

So, the shadows of God, for Nietzsche, are rationalist worldviews, whose common characteristic is the belief in determinate, unambiguous world-structuring principles. By the term *God,* then, Nietzsche refers to any such rational principle or set of principles, whether or not they take the form of a supernatural divine being. And Nietzsche's claim, "God is dead," is his affirmation of the world's irrationality, of the fundamental ambiguity described earlier—an ambiguity that results from the absence of any rational world-constituting principles, the absence of a "God." In other words, it is his affirmation of an existentialist ontology—in his case, that all existence is fundamentally will, unfulfillable self-transcendence.

That Nietzsche conceives of God in this manner explains his comparison of God with the sun, in which he claims that the death of God is analogous to the earth being unchained from the sun and so losing its direction. The Nietzschean God is analogous to the sun in the following way. Just as the sun sets and maintains the earth's motion through space on a formulable, calculable, determinate course, thereby playing the role of the earth's rational, motion-determining principle, so "God" gives determinate order to worldly occurrences, thereby playing the role of the rational, identity-determining principle of all existence. Without "God," then, the world lacks a determinate structuring principle—the world is irrational—just as, without the sun, the earth would lack a determinate principle of motion, and so would spin chaotically through space. Again, Nietzsche's proclamation of God's death is his affirmation of a disorderly, irrational world.

Our brief characterization of Nietzsche's irrational, ambiguous world of will draws a fundamental contrast between his own worldview and the worldviews that have dominated Western culture. Nietzsche simultaneously rejects the natural scientific worldview's belief in unbreakable laws of nature, the social scientific worldview's belief in laws of social development, and the religious worldview's belief in divine providence. All of these are expressions of Platonic rationalism's belief in determinate world-structuring principles, its belief in "God." To contrast his worldview with that of science and religion, Nietzsche sometimes describes it as an *aesthetic* worldview. This characterization allows us one more point of view from which to sketch Nietzsche's ontology.

Nietzsche characterizes his worldview as aesthetic insofar as it conceives the world as analogous to a work of art. Here, Nietzsche focuses on the fact that the creation of a work of art does not follow rules or formulas; there is no preestablished set of determinate directives for creating a work of art. Similarly, Nietzsche's world of will does not function in accordance with any determinate set of rules. And just as this lack of rules renders artworks ambiguous in the sense that their artistic character, their being better or worse instances of art, cannot be definitively determined, so the ontological identities of things in Nietzsche's world are ambiguous—their being better or worse instances of a thing of some particular type cannot be definitively determined. All existing things, from Nietzsche's point of view, inhabit the gray area of indeterminacy that we usually conceive as peculiar to the realm of art.

II. KIERKEGAARD'S ONTOLOGY—THE PRIMACY OF THE INDIVIDUAL

Søren Kierkegaard, like Nietzsche, viewed the world as devoid of determinate structuring principles, but, unlike Nietzsche, Kierkegaard was a devout Christian. Kierkegaard was primarily concerned with the way to live a good, properly Christian, life, and so a fuller treatment of Kierkegaard's thought will have to wait until our chapter on existentialist ethics. Still, Kierkegaard's position regarding the Christian life has ontological implications, which we will now examine. Most importantly, we must ask how Kierkegaard's belief in God does not prevent his world from holding fundamental similarities with Nietzsche's godless world of will. In other words, how is a Christian existentialism possible?

Whereas Nietzsche articulates the ambiguity of the world in terms of its ever-changing, self-transcendent nature, Kierkegaard expresses the world's ambiguity in terms of the individuality of its states. An understanding of Kierkegaard's emphasis on individuality, and of the way that this amounts to an affirmation of the world's ambiguity, can be gained by noting how Plato's ontology subordinates the individual to the universal.

In our introductory chapter, we saw that Platonic rationalism maintains that the world is composed of objects with determinate, unambiguous natures, or univocal conceptual identities, which make them what they are. Still, objects can seem to be ambiguous, as in the case of the beanbag chair, and we will now look more closely at the source of such apparent ambiguities. From a Platonic point of view, all objects possess two types of properties—those that determine them to be the types of things that they are and those that are irrelevant to their being the types of things that they are. The former have come to be known as essential properties, whereas the latter have been named accidental properties. To illustrate this, we can consider the case of a red chair. Insofar as such an object is a chair, it possesses the properties that determine a chair to be a chair; it has the essential chair properties. However, its possession of the property of being red is irrelevant to its being a chair because it would still be a chair if it were, say, blue. Thus, its being red does not determine it to be a chair, but is a merely accidental property.

Notice how the distinction between essential and accidental properties relates to the individuality of objects. Whereas the red chair's possession of the essential chair properties makes it a chair, these properties do not determine it to be the particular chair that it is because *all* chairs possess these properties, and so its possession of essential properties does not distinguish it from other chairs. Instead, the chair's possession of accidental properties performs the function of making it this particular chair; the accidental properties give the chair its individuality. For it is the particular chair that it is, rather than some other chair, because it is red, and, say, three feet tall, wooden, at this location in space, and so on. So, an object's accidental properties, the properties that are irrelevant to its belonging to the category of objects to which it belongs, distinguish it from others of its type. The essential properties of a thing, on the other hand, give it its universal, rather than individual, character. That is, because the essential properties are the properties that all things of a given type possess, they are what things of that type universally possess.

Insofar as accidental properties individualize objects, they also introduce ambiguity into objects. This can be seen by again considering the case of a red chair. Being a chair, it possesses the essential properties that make a chair a chair; it has all of the chair properties. These essential properties make it a chair, so the possession of essential properties gives the chair its univocal conceptual identity. To generalize the point, we can say that an X's essential properties are its X properties, and these properties make it a determinate object—an X. Along with its essential properties, the red chair has accidental properties, or properties that are not determinative of its being a chair, such as its being red and its position in space. These properties are irrelevant to its conceptual identity because it would be just as much a chair if it lacked them. Thus, insofar as the red chair is red, it is as much a chair as it is a non-chair. In this sense, the chair's accidental property of being red is not one of its chair properties, but is one of its non-chair properties, not in the sense that it prevents it from being a chair, but insofar as this property is, so to speak, chair-neutral. To again generalize, we can say that an X's essential properties are its X properties, whereas its accidental properties are its non-X properties.

We can now see how the possession of accidental properties besets objects with a kind of ambiguity or indeterminacy. Suppose an object had nothing but essential properties. Possessing only X properties, it would be completely unambiguous, completely determinate, with regard to the type of thing that it is; it would be a pure X. With the introduction of accidental properties, however, such an object would lose its purity. Possessing both essential and accidental properties, the object would have both X properties and non-X properties. The accidental properties introduce non-X properties into X's in that these properties give X's a non-X dimension along with the X dimension that constitutes them as X's. In this regard, objects with both essential and accidental properties are both X and non-X; they are *ambiguous*. And the world is populated by objects with both essential and accidental properties.

Notice that Plato's distinction between what were to be subsequently christened essential and accidental properties seems to conflict with his fundamentally rationalist doctrine of the world's determinacy, its univocity. For, as we can now see, accidental properties introduce ambiguity into the objects that possess them. With this problem in mind, we can see how the importance of Plato's prioritization of the universal over the individual comes into play. According to Plato, there are two types of objects in the universe: intelligible objects and sensible objects. Intelligible objects, or Forms, are composed of nothing but essential properties, whereas sensible objects are composed of both essential and accidental properties. And because the everyday world consists of objects of the latter type, Plato is compelled to posit another ontological realm in which to house the Forms. That is, with his two-tiered ontology, Plato intends to account for the apparent ambiguity of everyday sensible objects, while maintaining his rationalist claim that the world is fundamentally univocal. This can be seen by way of the following.

The Forms, being composed of essential properties alone, are pure types, and each sensible object is determined to be the type of object that it is by its corresponding Form. For instance, a particular chair possesses both chair and non-chair, essential and accidental, properties. Its possession of chair properties makes it a chair despite its simultaneous possession of non-chair properties. And it is the Form of chair-ness, which possesses only chair properties, that determines that such an object belongs to the category of chairs; the form determines which of an object's properties are essential and which are accidental. In other words, Forms determine the conceptual identities of sensible objects.

Now, Plato's basic rationalist claim is that sensible objects are deficient facsimiles of the Forms, whereas Forms serve as paradigms that the sensible objects unsuccessfully emulate. From the Platonic point of view, the true character of an object, say its being a chair, is found in its chair properties, its essential properties. Alternatively, its non-chair, or accidental, properties are its secondary aspects; they do not give it its true character. Thus, if the chair were not saddled with accidental properties, it would fully achieve itself; it would be, fully and purely, what it is. Hence, Plato's view of sensible objects as inferior versions of the Forms on which they are modeled. This hierarchy is made possible by Plato's two-tiered ontology insofar as it allows him to separate pure, unambiguous Forms from the ambiguous sensible objects that emulate them. This separation of Forms from their sensible instances, in turn, allows Plato to maintain that the world is determinate. That is, although sensible objects have properties that beset them with ambiguity, the true character of these objects, a character found in their corresponding Forms, is determinate, unambiguous.

Plato's prioritization of the Forms is a prioritization of the universal over the individual because, as we have seen, accidental properties give an object its individual character, whereas essential properties give it its universal character. And this universal character of an object is equivalent to its univocal, unambiguous character—the true nature of an object is its determinacy. The true character of the world, for Plato, is its unambiguous Form-determined nature. Ambiguities in the world are deficiencies that detract from its true character. To properly understand the world, then, we must focus on its properly univocal character, its universal characteristics, and ignore its apparent ambiguities, the individuality of things and situations. For example, supposing for the sake of argument that a beanbag chair really is a kind of chair, a proper understanding of this requires that we ignore the accidental properties that make it, specifically, a beanbag chair, and that thus individuate it as this particular chair. Instead, we are to focus on its essential chair properties because these properties are what make it what it truly is. We must ignore its individuality along with the ambiguities that this apparently introduces into the object. In this way, we will recognize that the world is, truly, determinate, unambiguous—rational.

We now turn to Kierkegaard. Unlike Plato, Kierkegaard prioritizes the individual. His prioritization of the individual focuses on the individuality of persons, but it also applies to the nature of the worldly situations in which human beings find themselves and the actions that they might perform in these situations. These issues, again, will become clearer in our chapter on existentialist ethics, but can now be addressed with regard to the ontological implications of the individuality of situations and actions. Kierkegaard's fundamental claim, here, is that the true character of worldly things and situations includes their accidental, individuating aspects; it, therefore, includes the characteristics that render the world ambiguous. Here, we can see how the existentialist revolt against Platonic rationalism leads to a subordination of abstract, general principles, in favor of concrete, individual phenomena. Platonic rationalism's prioritization of the universal, its exclusive focus on a thing's essential characteristics, is, for Kierkegaard, a mere abstraction that fails to consider that the accidental is just as much a part of any thing's identity as is the essential. Thus, the individual thing, which includes both types of properties, and is, for the reasons cited earlier, ambiguous, is the thing in its true character. The individual holds priority over the universal. Hence, the world, in its true character, is ambiguous, indeterminate—irrational.

Kierkegaard's paradigm example of the priority of the individual is found in the Biblical story of Abraham and Isaac. Kierkegaard's interest in this story issues from his belief that Abraham's view of the world, or the ontology that Abraham implicitly adopts, is the worldview of a true Christian, and that this worldview prioritizes the individual over the universal. For when God told Abraham to kill his son Isaac, Abraham recognized that this would be an act of murder, and thus a violation of ethical law. In other words, this act would meet all of the conditions required to classify an act as one of murder; it would possess all of the essential properties that make murders count as murders. However, Abraham also recognized that even though killing Isaac, with regard to its universal characteristics or essential properties, would be a murder, he would be justified in doing so because the particular circumstances in which the act was to take place would override the universal aspect of the proposed act. That is, what would have made this act the particular act that it would have been, had Abraham carried it out, must include its accidental, individuating characteristics—most importantly, that it was ordered by God. Thus, according to Kierkegaard, Abraham's willingness to kill Isaac reveals that he views the world as ambiguous, that he holds an existentialist ontology. And because Kierkegaard sees Abraham as the father of Christian faith, he concludes that such an ontology constitutes the worldview of the true Christian believer. A true Christian, for Kierkegaard, is an existentialist.

With this in mind, we can see how Kierkegaard combines belief in God with existentialist irrationalism. Recall that Nietzsche sees the belief in God as incompatible with existentialist ontology insofar as God is conceived as a determinate, unambiguous world-structuring principle. Undoubtedly, many of those who believe in God, Christian or otherwise, hold such a view because it certainly seems that God's goodness precludes God from fashioning an irrational world, an ambiguous world that our rational capacities would be incapable of understanding. Particularly, it seems that a benevolent God would not allow the situations in which we find ourselves to be *morally* ambiguous. For if that were the case, then no action would be univocally good or evil, and so there would be no way to rationally determine how we ought to act in a given situation. But Kierkegaard maintains that this is precisely the sort of world that God created, and he takes the aforementioned story of Abraham as his evidence for this view. That is, Abraham finds himself in a situation in which the determinate, unambiguous prohibition against murder is rendered ambiguous by the individuating characteristics of that situation.

Kierkegaard combines his irrationalist worldview with a belief in God by holding that although God does play the role of a world-structuring principle, that same God is *not* a determinate, unambiguous world-structuring principle. Instead, God Himself is an individual. As an individual, God does not have a univocal conceptual identity, but is saddled with the same indeterminacy that individuality confers on things in the world. And God's indeterminacy yields an ambiguous world because it makes God's world-structuring acts irrational. This can be seen by contrasting the world-structuring acts of an indeterminate God with those of a determinate, rational world-structuring principle.

Consider the way that the conceptual identity of determinate things is related to the states that such things can take on, or in other words, how possession of a univocal conceptual identity is related to the behavior of such things. The possession of a univocal identity sets restrictions on the behavior of a determinate thing. Its possession of such an identity, its being unambiguously a particular type of thing, prevents it from behaving in ways that are in conflict with being that type of thing. For instance, a chair cannot begin walking and talking because these behaviors conflict with what it is to be a chair. Put in terms of the distinction between essential and accidental properties, the chair cannot take on states, or behave in ways, that conflict with its essential properties. The reason is that because these are the properties that make it a chair, its behaving in ways that conflict with these properties would be equivalent to its losing these properties. Thus, for a chair to walk and talk would conflict with its essential property of being inanimate, and so would be equivalent to its losing this property. But if the chair were to lose any of its essential properties, it would lose its conceptual identity—it would lose the very determinacy that makes it the determinate thing that it is. To generalize the point, a determinate thing's behavior is restricted by its essential properties in the sense that its behavior can never result in the loss of any of these properties. A determinate thing's accidental properties, on the other hand, do not restrict its behavior because these properties are irrelevant to its conceptual identity, and so the thing in question may lose such properties without losing its identity.

We can now apply this analysis to the behavior of a determinate, rational world-structuring principle. Insofar as such a principle is determinate, its behavior is subject to certain rationally articulable restrictions or rules; specifically, rules prohibiting behavior that would conflict with its univocal conceptual identity. And because the function of such a principle is to give structure to the world, the rules in question would be rules guiding its world-structuring acts. These rule-governed acts, in turn, give the world its rational structure.

Consider, now, the behavior of an ambiguous, indeterminate thing. Lacking a univocal identity, such a thing is not constrained by rules; there is no behavior that could count as its losing its conceptual identity because it has no such identity to lose. Notice that this implies that the behavior, that is, the world-structuring acts, of an indeterminate world-structuring principle are not constrained by rules. And because, as we have seen, things considered in their individuality are indeterminate, the world-structuring acts of Kierkegaard's God are not constrained by rules because Kierkegaard conceives of God as an individual. This point can be understood more clearly by regarding it in terms of the distinction between essential and accidental properties.

We have seen that when a thing is conceived in its individuality, or when the individual is prioritized over the universal, its essential and accidental properties are seen as equally constitutive of that thing. In this sense, the individual thing is such that there is no real distinction between the two types of properties. That is, no mere subdivision of its properties gives it its true identity, but instead all of its properties are on equal ground in this regard. More specifically, all of its properties function as accidental properties. For the function of essential properties is to give things a univocal identity, but that of accidental properties is to individuate things. And the individual thing is, precisely, an individuated thing with no univocal identity, an indeterminate thing. This is why Kierkegaard's conceiving of God as an individual renders God devoid of rules according to which the world is structured—a thing's accidental properties do not restrict its behavior. Through this conception of God, then, Kierkegaard is able to maintain God's existence while maintaining an existentialist ontology, that is, the view of the world as indeterminate, irrational.

III. HEIDEGGER'S ONTOLOGY—THE INDETERMINACY OF BEING

Martin Heidegger's main philosophical preoccupation was to answer the question, What is being? That is, he endeavored to discover what, exactly, it is for something to be, or, in other words, to discover the fundamental structure of all that is. Heidegger approaches this question by way of the phenomenological method, which intends to derive the structure of existing things from the objects of immediate experience. That is, phenomenology attempts to read these fundamental structures from objects as they appear to us in our everyday commerce with them. And, according to Heidegger, such everyday objects are what he calls "ready-to-hand" things, by which he means objects of use.

Heidegger's claim is that when we look at our normal, immediate encounters with objects, we find them to be determined by the uses to which they can be put. What makes the object of immediate experience what it is is its specific usefulness. Heidegger defends this claim by taking a hammer as his paradigm example of an everyday object. And he notes that in our normal, immediate encounter with a hammer, we experience it as a thing with which to, say, drive nails. Thus, in immediate experience, to be a hammer is to be a thing with which to drive nails, that is, it is to be a thing with a certain use. Furthermore, Heidegger maintains that this characterization of our immediate experience of the hammer applies to our immediate encounters with all objects. So, to generalize the point, in immediate experience, to be a thing of a certain type is to have a certain use.

Here, it might be objected that Heidegger's characterization of the object of immediate experience as an object of use may be applicable to some objects, but not to all objects. That is, it seems that whereas objects such as hammers, which are produced specifically as tools, are indeed immediately experienced as determined by their uses, this does not seem to be the case with regard to things that are not so produced. The most obvious counter-examples to Heidegger's characterization would be natural objects, such as rocks. But even in this case, Heidegger's analysis is quite plausible because it could be easily argued that, in immediate experience, a rock is encountered not as, say, a mass of sedimented materials, but rather as, perhaps, something to throw at your brother, or to kick down the street, and so forth. With this example in mind, we can see how Heidegger's analysis can be applied to objects of all types.

Given Heidegger's characterization of the objects of immediate experience as objects of use, the next issue to be addressed concerns the fundamental structure of the object of use, the fundamental structure of the ready-to-hand. For, as we have seen, the phenomenological method used by Heidegger intends to read the fundamental structure of existing things per se from the fundamental structure of the object of immediate experience. And Heidegger arrives at the structure of the ready-to-hand by focusing on its relation to subjectivity. That is, he derives the nature of the everyday useful object from its relation to the everyday user thereof.

One aspect of the ready-to-hand object's relation to subjectivity is the dependence of the former upon the latter. We can see this by using the example of a chair. A chair is immediately experienced as a thing to sit on, the chair as ready-to-hand. To be a thing to sit on, then, is what it is to be a chair. And for there to be things to sit on, there must be possible sitters. Or, to generalize the point, there can be no useful things without possible users. In this sense, ready-to-hand objects are dependent upon subjectivity, or subject-dependent.

Insofar as the ready-to-hand is subject-dependent, subjectivity somehow makes it possible for the useful object to be what it is. In other words, subjectivity plays an active role in the constitution of everyday ready-to-hand things. Extrapolating, now, in accordance with the phenomenological method, from the fundamental structure of the object of immediate experience to that of things per se, Heidegger maintains that to be a thing is to be dependent upon, or constituted by, subjectivity. To be is to be essentially related to, or made possible by, subjectivity. In this sense, being is subject-dependence.

Notice the counter-intuitive nature of Heidegger's position thus far. Our common-sense belief regarding the relation between objects and subjectivity maintains that objects are essentially subject-*independent*. This position, often referred to as "common-sense realism," holds that objects are not constituted by subjectivity, but are what they are independently thereof. After all, it seems obvious that things would not lose their identities, or even change in any significant way, if there were suddenly nobody to experience them. Heidegger's position, however, is that, in view of the findings of immediate experience, the commonsense position is mistaken; subjectivity makes objects possible. To better understand Heidegger's assault on commonsense realism, we must now take a closer look at the way in which subjectivity constitutes objects.

Again, taking immediate experience as our guiding clue, we ask, How, exactly, does the user of the ready-to-hand make such objects possible? Returning to our previous example of a chair, recall that chairs are immediately experienced as things to sit on, and that subjectivity makes such things possible insofar as there cannot be things to sit on without possible sitters. And to be a possible sitter, one must be competent to sit, competent to use the chair. Thus, generally speaking, subjectivity makes the ready-to-hand possible by being competent to use the ready-to-hand. Heidegger makes this point by holding that subjectivity constitutes the ready-to-hand by understanding it. In other words, the object-constituting acts by which ready-to-hand objects are made possible are acts of understanding. Extrapolating, now, in accordance with the phenomenological method, from the fundamental structure of objects of immediate experience to that of things per se, we can conclude that, for Heidegger, subjectivity constitutes things per se by understanding what it is that makes things per se what they are, by understanding what makes a thing a thing. And to understand what makes a thing a thing is to understand what it is for a thing to be at all; it is to understand its being. Therefore, in Heidegger's terms, subjectivity, which Heidegger refers to as "Dasein," makes things, or "beings," possible through its understanding of being.

We have now arrived at one of the basic structural elements of anything that is. To be is to be subject-dependent, or Dasein-dependent, insofar as to be is to be understood by Dasein. Thus, we have taken the first step in answering the question that drives Heidegger's thought—the question that asks, What is being? Being, thus far, is Dasein-dependence. However, this Dasein-dependence is only one element of the being of beings. To see the other element, we must, again, consult immediate experience.

As we have seen, in our normal, immediate encounters with objects, we find them to be objects of use, and such objects depend on subjectivity for their uses. Still, this subject-dependence must be qualified in view of the fact that subjectivity cannot put ready-to-hand objects to any use that it pleases. That is, the useful things of immediate experience have a limited range of uses to which they can be put. For instance, a chair cannot be used as food, or as a writing implement, and so on. Such limitations qualify the subject-dependence of useful objects because if they were completely dependent upon subjectivity to be what they are, then they could be used for any arbitrary purpose that we might choose. That their uses, and thus their identities, are limited, implies that the useful objects of immediate experience possess, along with their subject-dependence, an aspect that is beyond subjectivity's object-constituting power, that is, a subject-independent dimension.

Insofar as the ready-to-hand is subject-independent, subjectivity is not required for the useful object to be what it is; it is what it is apart from any relation it might have to subjectivity. In other words, the subject-independence of the ready-to-hand object implies that subjectivity does not play an active role in the constitution of useful things, but instead that in its normal encounters with everyday objects, subjectivity must passively conform to the uses to which such objects allow themselves to be put. Extrapolating, now with this aspect of the ready-to-hand in mind and in accordance with the phenomenological method, from the fundamental structure of the object of immediate experience to that of things per se, Heidegger maintains that to be a thing is to be independent from, or constituted without, subjectivity. To be is to be essentially alien to, not made possible by, subjectivity. In this sense, being is subject-independence.

Notice the problematic character of the position to which Heidegger's analysis has led us. On the one hand, his explication of the structure of the object of immediate experience, that is, of the ready-to-hand, shows that such objects are subject-dependent because they must be understood by subjectivity to be what they are, and so, in this sense, are constituted by subjectivity. This leads Heidegger to maintain that the fundamental structure, or being, of objects per se is their Dasein-dependence. Specifically, beings are constituted by Dasein insofar as the latter must understand the being of beings for them to be. However, Heidegger's analysis also shows that the ready-to-hand is subject-independent because the determinations that make such things what they are cannot be arbitrarily forged by subjectivity,

and so such determinations, and the ready-to-hand objects constituted thereby, are what they are without subjectivity; ready-to-hand
objects do not require subjectivity's acts of object-constitution. This
leads Heidegger to maintain that the fundamental structure, or being,
of objects per se is their Dasein-independence. Specifically, beings are
not constituted by Dasein insofar as they do not require that the latter
understand their being for them to be. Combining these two aspects
of the structure of beings, we are left in a position in which objects
are both Dasein-dependent and Dasein-independent, in which
objects are constituted by Dasein's understanding of being and, at
the same time, are not constituted thereby—a position in which
Dasein is itself both active and passive in its relation to objects.
How does Heidegger reconcile these equally essential, but apparently
incompatible, aspects of things? To answer this question, we must first
examine the precise relation between the ready-to-hand's subject-
dependent and subject-independent elements, between everyday subjectivity's active and passive dimensions.

Returning to our normal, immediate encounters with ready-to-
hand objects, notice that the everyday subject's involvements with
such useful things aims at overcoming the subject-independent
dimension of the ready-to-hand. That is, subjectivity's acts of
object-use would reach a state of perfection if all traces of the object's
resistance to such acts were to disappear. For if this were to occur,
ready-to-hand objects would be fully responsive to subjectivity; being
completely under our control, they would submit to our every whim.
That this is what the everyday subject's use-acts take as their goal can
be seen by noting the frustration that accompanies our meeting
resistance in objects. To be a fully achieved, or consummate, object
user, then, would amount to being involved with the ready-to-hand
in such a way that such objects never frustrated, or resisted, our acts of
use—a life in which all of our endeavors were immediately satisfied.

Although the everyday subject's activities are driven by its
attempt to achieve itself by overcoming the subject-independent
dimension of the ready-to-hand, this is an impossible goal, impossible
not merely in fact but in principle. For the subject-independence of
the ready-to-hand is essential to its being what it is; it is part of its
fundamental ontological structure. At the same time, if subjectivity
were to achieve itself, subjectivity itself would lose its passive dimension. For as consummate user of useful objects, the acts by which it
uses the ready-to-hand would be equivalent to acts by which it
constitutes the ready-to-hand because such objects would completely

submit to the uses to which subjectivity arbitrarily chose to put them. Using an object in any given way would make the object into a thing whose identity is determined by its being used in precisely that way. This is impossible because everyday subjectivity is not an omnipotent, purely active object-constituting power of this sort. Instead, its passive dimension is part of its fundamental ontological structure.

So, the relation between subjectivity's active and passive dimensions is one in which it is constantly trying to become purely active, to overcome its own passive dimension. But this can never be achieved because it would no longer be subjectivity if it were to accomplish this task. Everyday subjectivity, then, is in principle unachievable. That is, insofar as subjectivity, for Heidegger, aims at an in principle impossible goal, it is indeterminate for the same reason, and thus in the same way, that Nietzschean will to power is. Subjectivity is self-transcendent, continually attempting to achieve itself, but its goal of self-achievement cannot be grasped in any determinate formula. A fully achieved subject both is and is not what it is—as self-achieved *subjectivity,* it possesses both passive and active dimensions, but as *self-achieved* subjectivity, it is purely active. And so, resisting any determinate, rational formulation of its self-achievement, everyday object-using subjectivity is ontologically indeterminate, ambiguous.

We are now prepared to note the relation between the ready-to-hand object's subject-dependent and subject-independent dimensions, and thus to ultimately answer the question asked earlier, concerning Heidegger's reconciliation of these two, equally essential, but apparently incompatible, aspects of things. To do this, we must first take a closer look at the impossibility of subjectivity's achieving itself as consummate object-user.

Recall, here, the precise character of the acts by which subjectivity constitutes the ready-to-hand. Subjectivity, as we have seen, makes the ready-to-hand possible by understanding it. With this in mind, the previous analysis implies that the ready-to-hand is structured in such a way that it cannot be fully understood. That is, because subjectivity constitutes ready-to-hand objects by understanding them, its continual attempt to achieve itself as consummate object-user, to become a fully active constituting agent of the ready-to-hand, is equivalent to its attempt to fully understand the ready-to-hand. And because subjectivity can never fully constitute such useful objects, although it continually strives to do so, it follows that subjectivity can never fully understand the ready-to-hand. This refusal to allow subjectivity to understand it completely is ingredient to the fundamental structure of the useful object;

specifically, the ready-to-hand's resistance to being fully understood is a function of its essential subject-independent dimension. The ready-to-hand, then, being beyond the scope of any determinate, articulable formula, being beyond the grasp of rational thought, is ontologically indeterminate, ambiguous. In other words, the basic structure of the ready-to-hand, what it is to be ready-to-hand, is to be indeterminate.

Notice what our latest look into the structure of everyday experience reveals about the seemingly incompatible aspects of everyday objects and of everyday subjectivity. It shows that Heidegger reconciles the subject-dependence and subject-independence of everyday objects, as well as the activity and passivity of the everyday subject, by acknowledging that these apparent incompatibilities imply that both the ready-to-hand and the user thereof are indeterminate. And, in keeping with the phenomenological method, Heidegger further concludes that the fundamental structure of Dasein and of objects per se is one of indeterminacy. We can understand how this works in the following way.

Beginning with everyday subjectivity, we have seen that the user of the ready-to-hand is driven toward the overcoming of its passive dimension, toward achieving itself as a fully active constituting agent of the ready-to-hand, and that such self-achievement would be tantamount to its gaining a full understanding of the ready-to-hand. We have also seen that such self-achievement is in principle impossible because it would require that everyday subjectivity lose its essential passive dimension, and so the everyday subject is fundamentally indeterminate. Extrapolating, now, in accordance with the phenomenological method, from the fundamental structure of the subject of immediate experience to that of subjectivity per se, that is, of Dasein, we can conclude that, for Heidegger, Dasein is indeterminate. That is, Dasein is driven toward the overcoming of its passive dimension, toward achieving itself as fully active constituting agent of objects per se, and such self-achievement would be tantamount to gaining a full understanding of being. But such self-achievement is in principle impossible because it would require that Dasein lose its essential passive dimension, and so Dasein is, fundamentally, indeterminate. This is Heidegger's ultimate, phenomenologically derived conclusion regarding the basic structure of subjectivity. Thus, Heidegger argues that Dasein, being indeterminate or ambiguous, has no univocal conceptual identity. In this sense, Heidegger's analysis yields an existentialist conception of human subjectivity.

Turning now to Heidegger's conception of the nature of objects, we have seen that everyday subjectivity's ineluctable failure to fully understand the ready-to-hand indicates that the ready-to-hand is structured in such a way as to resist being completely understood. Thus, the ready-to-hand is beyond the scope of rational thought; to be ready-to-hand is to be indeterminate. Extrapolating, now, in accordance with the phenomenological method, from the fundamental structure of the objects of immediate experience to that of objects per se, we can conclude that being is indeterminate. That is, Dasein's ineluctable failure to fully understand objects indicates that they are structured in such a way as to resist being completely understood. Thus, objects are beyond the scope of rational thought; to be an object is to be indeterminate. Heidegger, then, argues that objects, being indeterminate or ambiguous, have no univocal conceptual identity. Put in more Heideggerian terms, the basic structure of beings, what it is to be, is to be indeterminate; being is indeterminate. Hence, Heidegger's existentialist ontology with regard to both human subjectivity and the world of objects.

IV. SARTRE'S ONTOLOGY—THE PRECEDENCE OF EXISTENCE

Jean-Paul Sartre's ontology is, perhaps, best approached through his famous statement that, for the human being, existence precedes essence. With this statement, Sartre draws a distinction between two categories of things, or two ways of being. The two types of things, in Sartre's ontology, are those that are conscious, whose way of being he names "being for itself," and those that are not conscious, whose way of being he names "being in itself." Sartre maintains that conscious beings are structured in such a way that their existence precedes their essence, whereas beings that do not possess consciousness are structured in such a way that their essence precedes their existence. And because he sees human beings as the only conscious beings, we can understand the characterization, concerning the relation between existence and essence, by examining the way that he conceives the nature of human consciousness.

Like Heidegger, Sartre was a phenomenologist—he derives the basic structure of consciousness from an examination of the way that consciousness appears in normal, immediate experience. In his analysis of such experience, Sartre focuses on the fact that consciousness is always conscious of both an object and of itself. His focusing on that which consciousness is conscious of follows from the preliminary notion of consciousness that he inherits from the founder of phenomenology: Edmund Husserl. Husserl had noted that the most basic characteristic of consciousness is that it is intentional, by which he meant that it is always directed at, or always intends, something. Simply put, consciousness is always consciousness of ...; a consciousness that is not conscious *of* something is no consciousness at all.

Returning to what, exactly, consciousness is of, or what it intends, Sartre maintains that it is conscious of an object and of itself. Beginning with the former, we should note that Sartre's claim is not that we are necessarily conscious of external objects; after all, we can be conscious of thoughts, dream-images, and all sorts of phenomena that are internal to our minds. Thus, the claim that consciousness is always of an object counts both internal and external phenomena as "objects." Ultimately, to say that consciousness is always of an object is simply to say that consciousness is necessarily directed at something—the principle of the intentionality of consciousness mentioned previously.

At the same time that consciousness is always of an object, it is also, Sartre claims, consciousness of itself, specifically, consciousness of itself as that which is conscious of the object. That is, consciousness is always conscious of itself insofar as it never confuses itself with the object toward which it is directed, but always notices that its object is different than consciousness itself. For example, a moment ago I looked at the notebook on which I am writing. At that moment, my consciousness was directed at, or intended, the notebook. I was explicitly aware of the notebook, or as Sartre puts it, I was positionally conscious of it. But although I was positionally conscious of the notebook, I was also aware that I was not the notebook, and so was conscious not only of the notebook, but of myself as well. Hence, Sartre's claim that consciousness is always conscious both of an object and of itself.

A pivotal point to note, here, is that, in normal experience, the self-consciousness that accompanies all consciousness of objects is not an explicit self-consciousness. To see this, consider, again, my intending of the notebook. As I looked at the notebook, I was aware that I was not it, but I was not overtly thinking about that fact. That is, whereas I was not thinking something like, "Here is a notebook, and here *I* am, sitting in this chair, looking at the notebook," and so forth; I was thinking something like, "Here is a notebook," and I was implicitly noting, "I am not it." To generalize the point, consciousness is normally immersed in its objects, explicitly intending them, absorbed in the world toward which it is directed; and it is also conscious of itself, but merely implicitly, or as Sartre puts it, non-positionally. Therefore, Sartre holds that in normal, immediate experience, consciousness is positionally conscious of an object and non-positionally conscious of itself.

Recall that the point of Sartre's analysis is to discover the basic structure of consciousness. That is, Sartre analyzes the way that consciousness normally appears in immediate experience to derive the fundamental structure of consciousness therefrom. And, now, we can see how, according to Sartre, consciousness so appears—that is, as that which is not the object explicitly intended by consciousness. More specifically, it is not the explicitly intended object, but is rather that which does the intending; it is not what consciousness is explicitly of, but rather is that which is conscious of the object. This brings us to Sartre's pivotal claim regarding the nature of consciousness.

According to Sartre, consciousness experiences itself, in immediate experience, as lacking any content. We can understand this claim by recalling our example of my looking at my notebook. As we saw, I was aware of myself as I looked at the notebook, but I was not thinking about any of the properties that make me the specific person that I am. I was not noting that I am this person, sitting in this chair, nor that I was wearing these clothes, that I have this life history, and so on. Ultimately, I was aware of myself only as the one conscious of the object, without any characteristics beyond that. And, as no more than that which is conscious of the object, as simply consciousness, the self that I was aware of had no content. To generalize the point, consciousness appears, in normal, immediate experience, as devoid of content. Extrapolating, now, in accordance with the phenomenological method, from the fundamental structure of consciousness as it appears in immediate experience to that of consciousness as such, we can conclude that, for Sartre, consciousness is devoid of content.

At this point, it could be objected that self-consciousness is not necessarily non-positional, but instead that consciousness is capable of experiencing itself positionally, as possessing content, and that it often does so in normal experience. Specifically, consciousness apparently attains explicit consciousness of itself by shifting its attention away from objects and back onto itself. For example, as I look at my notebook, I am positionally aware of the notebook, focusing on it and noting the properties that make it this particular notebook; as I do this, I am also, as we have seen, non-positionally aware of myself.

However, I can then shift the direction of my awareness, and thereby direct my consciousness at, or intend, not the notebook but myself as the one who has been explicitly conscious of the notebook. When I do this, my consciousness of myself becomes positional; I become aware of myself not simply as the one who is conscious of an object, but as this person, sitting in this chair, wearing these clothes, possessing this life history, and so forth. In view of this fact, it seems that consciousness does have content; it simply requires a distinctive type of conscious act to notice this. And, if this is the case, then Sartre's extrapolation, in accordance with the phenomenological method, from the fundamental structure of consciousness as it appears in immediate experience to that of consciousness as such, would have to conclude that consciousness is not devoid of content.

Sartre was well aware of our ability to intend ourselves positionally. He refers to such acts of consciousness as reflective because they occur when consciousness reflects on itself. But, he argues, in acts of reflection, consciousness only seems to possess content, although it really does not. His argument for this claim turns on the fact that when consciousness performs an act of reflection, it does become aware of a self with content, but this self is not really consciousness at all. We can understand this by way of the following considerations.

Suppose that I were to reflect on myself as the one intending my notebook. At first glance, it may seem that the object of my reflection—myself—is equivalent to the consciousness that is performing the act of reflection. However, the self that I am thus conscious of is a bygone moment of consciousness; it is the consciousness that was intending the notebook before the act of reflection. Now, this past moment of consciousness is grasped positionally, and thus as possessing content. I am aware that, at that moment, I was this person, sitting in this chair, intending this notebook. But in the act of reflection that grasps this bygone, content-laden self, the consciousness that is reflectively aware of this past moment is itself grasped only non-positionally. Reflective consciousness itself is only noticed as that which is not the past moment of consciousness that is the object of the act of reflection; reflective consciousness itself appears not as the intended object, but as that which does the intending, that which is conscious of the object. At the moment of reflection, then, reflective consciousness is devoid of content. That is, just as in cases of non-reflective consciousness, such as my intending the notebook, consciousness is grasped non-positionally, and thus as without content; so in cases of reflective consciousness, such as intending myself as consciousness of the notebook, consciousness lacks content. Hence, the phenomenological warrant for Sartre's claim that consciousness as such is devoid of content.

Sartre expresses the lack of content, or emptiness, of consciousness in a number of ways, for example, by saying that consciousness is a *nothingness*. This lack of content is also expressed, by Sartre, in the claim with which we began our consideration of Sartre's thought, that is, that, for the human being, or the being that possesses consciousness, existence precedes essence. To understand how being devoid of content is equivalent to a precedence of existence over essence, we must first take note of the notion of essence that is at work in Sartre's claim. This notion is easily understood by recalling the distinction between essential and accidental properties discussed previously. As we have seen, the essential properties of a thing are the properties that determine it to be the type of thing that it is, that give it its conceptual identity. The essence of a thing is the combination of those essential properties; the essence, then, is what gives a thing its conceptual identity.

In view of Sartre's conception of consciousness as empty, as devoid of content, it follows that consciousness has no essence. For, lacking any content at all, it has no properties, and so cannot have any essential properties. Still, although consciousness is empty, or a nothingness, it is not nothing at all. It *is* consciousness; it exists. Possessing existence, then, consciousness is pure existence without essence. Such is the fundamental character of what is simply that which is conscious of . . ., that is, the fundamental character of human subjectivity.

But if consciousness is empty existence without essence, then why does Sartre claim that, for human subjectivity, existence *precedes* essence? Does this latter claim not imply that the human subject has an essence, even if this essence is posterior to, and thus subordinated to, the subject's sheer existence? We can understand the ultimate equivalence of Sartre's apparently conflicting characterizations of human subjectivity by first examining the relation between essence and existence in nonconscious things. And Sartre claims that, for such things, in direct contrast to human beings, their essence precedes their existence.

Sartre illustrates the precedence of essence over existence in nonconscious things by focusing on produced objects. For a thing to be produced, its producer must first conceive the thing to be produced; the producer must have the nature of the thing in mind before producing it. For example, a chair can only be produced if its maker first conceives what it is for a chair to be a chair, or what makes a chair a chair. And because the nature of a thing, that which makes it the type of thing that it is, is its essence, we can say that a producer must have the thing's essence in mind before producing the thing. Therefore, because the producer of a produced thing brings it into existence, Sartre concludes that, in the case of produced objects, their essence precedes their existence.

The precedence of essence over existence in produced things can be taken in two ways. On the one hand, we can say that, in such things, their essence precedes their existence in time, or temporally. This is the type of precedence on which Sartre focuses in his analysis of produced objects. That is, the essence of the thing to be produced must be in the mind of the producer before the thing is produced, before it exists. But his analysis also points to another, more important, type of precedence—what we will call an ontological precedence of essence over existence. That is, in produced things, their essence precedes their existence not only insofar as the essence of such things must exist in the minds of their producers before they exist, but also insofar as produced things are structured in such a way that their essence is more fundamental than their existence. The essence of a produced thing is more fundamental than, and so ontologically precedes, its existence in the sense that the thing's essence could be without there being any things embodying that essence, but not vice versa. For example, there could be chairness without there being any chairs. By contrast, there could be no things of a given type without there being an essence that they embody. The essence makes the thing the type of thing that it is, thereby making things of that type possible. Therefore, insofar as the existence of a produced thing depends unilaterally upon its essence, its essence precedes its existence *ontologically,* or by virtue of the fundamental structure of the thing in question.

Notice that the ascription of an ontological precedence of essence over existence applies not only to produced objects, but to objects in general. Whether an object was ever brought into existence through an act of production, its existence is unilaterally dependent upon its essence, for the reasons described earlier. The one exception to this rule, according to Sartre, is the human being, and the human being's possession of consciousness gives its existence priority over its essence. To understand this claim, we must look more closely at Sartre's view of the human being's basic structure.

As mentioned earlier, Sartre sees the possession of consciousness as distinctive of the human being. More particularly, he typically equates the human being with consciousness. This is what allows him to conclude that the emptiness of consciousness, its being no more than that which is conscious of . . ., implies that the human being is devoid of content, and so is without essence. But if the human being's existence precedes its essence, then it must also possess an essence in some sense.

The sense in which the human being has content, and thus an essence, can be understood by noting that Sartre conceives the human being as having two distinct aspects, and that he prioritizes one of these aspects over the other. Specifically, one aspect of the human being is consciousness, and a second aspect of the human being is what Sartre calls the ego. The ego is the self insofar as it has content, that is, insofar as the human being accrues properties throughout the course of its existence. That there is such a self is discovered through the acts of reflection that were discussed earlier. For the properties, or pieces of content, that the human being accrues are those characteristics that are explicitly grasped, positionally intended, in acts of reflection; they are the properties that make a given human being this particular human being. The ego is the self that possesses such properties; broadly put, the ego is the self that possesses a life history.

So, for Sartre, the two aspects of the human being are the following: empty, contentless consciousness and the content-laden ego. Sartre also prioritizes consciousness over the ego; consciousness is the genuine self, the true human subject, but the human being is an ego in a merely secondary way. He maintains this subordination of the ego because he sees the ego as the result of acts performed by consciousness. That is, consciousness is the source of the actions by which the human being gains a life history, by which the human being gives content to, or develops, its ego. For instance, I may construct an ego characterized by stinginess through acts in which I consistently refuse to spend money, thereby giving myself the life history, and thus the content, of a stingy person. I develop a stingy ego. That these ego-constituting acts are acts of consciousness can be seen by noting that when I perform an action, the self performing the action appears as devoid of content; the self is grasped non-positionally. For instance, as I perform an act of stinginess, say, leaving a poor tip for a waiter, I am positionally conscious of the tip itself—I am thinking something like, "Here is the small sum of money." At the same time, I am aware that I am not the tip, and so I am conscious of myself, but in a non-positional way; I am aware of myself simply as that which is performing the act of leaving the paltry tip. As in the case analyzed earlier of looking at the notebook, so in the case of performing acts that make me the sort of person that I am, such as acts of stinginess, I am absorbed in the world, and so I am aware of myself in a merely implicit way. That is, again, the self that I am conscious of has no content. In this case, the self that has no content is the self that performs the ego-constituting act. Thus, it is empty, contentless consciousness that acts, and thereby constructs an ego. Consciousness is the source of the actions by which the human being gains a life history, and so holds a position of priority over the ego that such actions construct.

Furthermore, not only does consciousness hold the power to construct the ego, but this power is unrestricted. Consciousness, according to Sartre, can construct for itself any ego that it chooses. This unrestrictedness of the human being's ego-constituting power follows from the lack of essence characteristic of consciousness. This can be seen by recalling that the essence of a thing restricts its behavior insofar as the states that a thing can take on cannot be states that are tantamount to its losing any of its essential properties. Therefore, consciousness, being devoid of all content and thus of any essential properties, could not act in a way that strips it of such properties because it never possessed any in the first place. Instead, consciousness can act in any arbitrary way, and so its ego-constituting ability has no restrictions. Thus, although the ego that I have constituted at this point in my life may be that of a stingy person, there is no reason that I could not, at any moment, begin acting in a non-stingy way, that I could not begin constructing an ego that conflicts with the ego that I have constructed until this point. For the consciousness that performs such ego-constituting acts is separate from the ego; it is the ego's source, and so it continues to lack any restrictive content even though its acts yield a content-laden self. No matter how many acts of stinginess a given consciousness may perform, and so no matter how much stinginess-content the ego constructed by that consciousness may accrue, the consciousness in question remains without content of its own. Consciousness, then, is able to reconstruct its ego at any moment. Even if I have been stingy throughout my entire life, the intrinsic emptiness of my consciousness allows me, suddenly, to engage in acts of generosity regardless of my past pattern of stinginess.

With this picture of the two aspects of the human being and of the relation between these aspects in mind, we can now understand why Sartre claims both that the human being is without essence and that the human being's existence precedes its essence. The human being lacks an essence insofar as the human being is equivalent to consciousness. And because consciousness is what the human being primarily is, Sartre can legitimately characterize the human being as empty, content-free, pure existence without essence. However, the acts of the human being thus characterized always generate a content-laden ego, and this ego is an aspect of the human being, although it is a merely secondary aspect because of its unilateral dependence upon consciousness. The human being's possession of content in the form of an ego gives the human being an essence in the following sense.

Because a thing's essence is composed of the properties that determine the thing to be a thing of a particular type, and because the properties accrued by a human being's ego make that person a particular type of person, for example, a stingy one, Sartre can say that the human being has a kind of essence. That is, the human being has an essence to the extent that it possesses content that makes it a particular type of human being.

The secondary character of the human being's ego, of its essence, qualifies the sense in which such content counts as an essence. This is because the secondary character of the ego refers to its being the product of an empty consciousness. This results in the malleability of the ego described earlier, the fact that consciousness can replace any of the ego's content, at any moment, by completely opposed pieces of content because the emptiness of consciousness leaves its ego-constituting acts completely unrestricted. The emptiness of consciousness, then, gives the human essence a revisability that essences typically disallow. In fact, the very purpose of essences is to prevent such radical revisions in the things that possess them because the crucial difference between essential and accidental properties lies in the fact that the essential properties of a thing are the properties that it necessarily possesses to be the type of thing that it is. The essence is, precisely, the unrevisable aspect of a thing. Thus, the human being only possesses an essence in a qualified, or secondary, sense because its essence is produced by the unrestricted acts of a contentless, that is, essenceless, consciousness, and so none of its content is unrevisable.

We can now understand Sartre's statement that, for human beings, their existence precedes their essence—the statement with which we began our examination of Sartre's ontology. With regard to the temporal precedence of existence over essence, recall that in the case of nonhuman, nonconscious produced things, such as chairs, the temporal precedence of essence over existence referred to the fact that such a thing's essence had to be in the mind of its producer before the thing was produced and thus existed. The human being, conversely, gains an essence, an ego, through acts of consciousness. That is, consciousness produces its ego, which implies that consciousness predates its essence. And because consciousness is pure existence without essence, the human being's existence comes before, or temporally precedes, its essence. In other words, the human being as consciousness temporally precedes the human being as ego. Because of the temporal precedence of existence over essence, according to Sartre and according to common sense, a newborn baby is not yet any particular type of person. At birth, the human being is sheer existence. And the type of person that the newborn will become is completely in his or her hands; it is to be determined by his or her acts of consciousness. Thus, for Sartre, we make ourselves into the type of person that we are. With regard to the ontological precedence of existence over essence, recall that in the case of nonhuman, nonconscious things, the ontological precedence of essence over existence referred to the fact that such a thing's existence is unilaterally dependent upon its essence. In the case of the human being, the relation of dependence between existence and essence is reversed because the human being's essence, its ego, is generated by, and thus is unilaterally dependent upon, consciousness, which is itself pure existence without essence.

To summarize, the precedence of the human being's existence over its essence results from the human being's lack of an essence. That is, because the human being (as consciousness) has no essence, the human being (as ego) only has an essence in a qualified, or secondary, sense. And because the possession of an essence in this qualified sense is the possession of content that is generated by a contentless, pure existence, a thing whose essence is secondary is a thing whose existence precedes its essence, both temporally and ontologically.

Our examination has now given us a clear picture of the two types of things in Sartre's ontology. The first is the human being, or that whose way of being is being for itself, whose existence precedes its essence. The second type of thing in Sartre's ontology is the nonhuman thing, or that whose way of being is being in itself, whose essence precedes its existence. Because of this precedence of essence, nonhuman things possess essences in an unqualified sense—properties that determine them to be the types of things that they are, and that restrict the behavior of the things that possess them. With our characterizations of these two types of things, we can understand the sense in which Sartre's ontology is an existentialist ontology.

The human being, as understood by Sartre, possesses the indeterminate, ambiguous structure that is characteristic of the existentialist's world because it lacks a univocal conceptual identity. The
human being is primarily essence-free, empty consciousness, having
no content that could determine it to be a particular type of thing. As
pure existence, consciousness is sheer indeterminacy, a nothingness; it
has no univocal conceptual identity. On the other hand, the human
being is also an ego, which is not a purely indeterminate nothingness,
but which possesses content that, apparently, gives it a determinate
character, makes it a determinate type of human being, say, a stingy
person rather than a generous one. Still, the determinacy of the ego is
not equivalent to a univocal conceptual identity, to determinacy in
the sense proper to a rationalist worldview. To understand this, we
must recall the role that such an identity plays in the behavior of fully
determinate, rational things.

As we have seen, the possession of a univocal conceptual identity
sets restrictions on the behavior of a thing that possesses such an
identity because having an identity of this sort, being unambiguously
a particular type of thing, prevents it from taking on states that
conflict with being a thing of that type. However, the ego's identity,
its type of determinacy, does not restrict its behavior because of its
being the product of acts of empty consciousness, because of the
secondary character of its content, its essence. In this way, the
indeterminacy of consciousness renders the ego, ultimately, indeterminate; the human being, then, is indeterminate, ambiguous in its
ontological structure. Hence, Sartre's view of the human subject is
clearly irrationalist, existentialist. Nonhuman things, however, possessing essences in an unqualified sense, are unambiguous. This determinacy of nonhuman objects seems to leave Sartre in a less radically
irrationalist position than are those of the other philosophers examined in this chapter. But, as we will see in the next chapter, the far-
reaching effects of Sartre's irrationalist conception of the human being
come to the fore in his ethical thought.

V. EXISTENTIALIST ONTOLOGY

In our introductory chapter, we defined existentialism as a kind of
irrationalism. Specifically, it is the denial of Platonic rationalism,
which maintains that things in the world are conceptually univocal,

that things are what they are in accordance with rational, or unambiguous, structuring principles. Thus, the basic claim of Platonic rationalist ontology is that to be is to be determinate. For the Platonic rationalist, then, the world can be completely understood; the nature of the world and the things that populate it can be fully grasped by way of determinate, articulable formulas.

We have now seen four paradigm examples of existentialist ontologies, of ontologies maintaining that there are no rational, unambiguous world-structuring principles, and thus that to be is to be indeterminate, ambiguous: irrational. Nietzsche attempts to capture the indeterminacy of the world by characterizing all existence as will to power, as unfulfillable self-transcendence—pure striving toward an indeterminate goal. Nietzsche arrives at this characterization by focusing on the fact that things in the world are constantly changing, constantly in flux. Kierkegaard's ontology of indeterminacy focuses on the individuality of all that exists, and maintains that existing things, when viewed as primarily individual, are fundamentally ambiguous. This conception of existence, Kierkegaard believes, lies at the heart of the Christian worldview. Heidegger derives the indeterminacy of both human subjectivity and the being of things through the phenomenological method, and he finds that the former is ambiguous insofar as it can never achieve itself as a fully active object-constituting agent, whereas the latter is ambiguous insofar as it can never be fully understood. Finally, Sartre uses the phenomenological method to argue that the human subject is without content, and so lacks a univocal conceptual identity.

Here, it should be noted that the four philosophers whose ontologies we have examined do not all maintain that the world is completely without identity. Such a world would be completely beyond the grasp of any kind of thought, completely meaningless. Instead, Nietzsche, Kierkegaard, and Heidegger hold that although the world lacks a univocal identity, it does have a kind of identity—an indeterminate one. That is, although the world is not structured by determinate principles, it still admits of structuring principles, whether such principles be thought as Nietzsche's will to power, Kierkegaard's individual God, or Heidegger's being. Sartre's case requires a closer examination, which will be carried out in our next chapter. In any case, we can conclude that just because existence cannot be understood by way of the determinate formulas of rational thought does not imply that it is simply without structure, and so beyond all cognition. Rather, the existentialists present the philosopher with a new challenge, that is, to approach existence through a type of cognition that does not employ rigid formulas but recognizes the ambiguity of existence, a type of cognition that is geared to indeterminacy. Briefly put, existentialism can be seen as endorsing a type of cognition that exhibits the flexibility of Platonic right opinion rather than the rigidity of Platonic knowledge.

To conclude this chapter, let us note the negative and positive consequences of existentialist ontology. In our introductory chapter, we noted that existentialism is commonly regarded as a pessimistic, destructive philosophy because its rejection of the world's rationality undermines some of Western culture's most basic institutions, such as science. We can now see how the rejection of science is implied by an existentialist ontology. The very purpose of science is to discover and articulate the fundamental laws in accordance with which the world functions, in accordance with which the world is what it is. And this project presupposes that there are such graspable, formulable laws—it presupposes that the world is rational, or determinate, in precisely the sense that existentialist ontology denies. This denial of the possibility of scientific knowledge, then, is one of the negative consequences of existentialism.

However, something positive also follows from the existentialist rejection of science; specifically, the aforementioned challenge to discover a type of cognition that is geared to the indeterminacy of the world, a type of cognition that is not held to the standards of exactitude demanded by scientific knowledge. This may seem to be just another of the negative consequences of existentialism, rather than a positive consequence. That is, the type of cognition allowed by an indeterminate world might appear to be a lower form of cognition than is scientific knowledge, because of the inexactitude of the former. This is precisely why Plato prioritized knowledge over right opinion. Thus, it seems that the existentialist's search for a non-scientific type of cognition is no more than an admission of our own cognitive inadequacies, and there is nothing positive about that.

But a closer look reveals that the existentialist's admission of the ultimate inexactitude of our knowledge is something positive because it would only be an admission of cognitive inadequacy if scientific exactitude captured the true nature of the world, which existentialist ontology denies. That is, if the world were determinate, as the Platonic rationalist claims, then an inexact form of cognition, such as right opinion, would be inadequate because its inexactitude, its indeterminacy, would amount to no more than a failure to understand the world, a failure to grasp the world's true, unambiguous nature. But existentialism denies that the world is, in fact, determinate, and so it maintains that the exact formulas by which the Platonist scientist attempts to understand the world are but falsifications of the world's true, ambiguous nature. Thus, the existentialist's rejection of science is a positive consequence of existentialist ontology insofar as it leads to the search for a type of cognition that captures the true nature of the world.

2

Ethics

I. THE PROBLEM OF
AN EXISTENTIALIST ETHICS

Although existentialism's subordination of exact knowledge to an inexact, ambiguous type of cognition, and the rejection of science that this implies, is undoubtedly problematic, the ethical consequences of the existentialist's adoption of an ontology of indeterminacy present a more obviously serious problem. To see why this is the case, recall that Plato prioritized the life of knowledge over the life of right opinion because knowledge would allow us to infallibly classify objects and actions; it is designed to take the guesswork, and thus the fallibility, out of our attempts to classify. And, as was noted in our introductory chapter, there seems to be much more at stake in our ethical classifications, in our classifying actions as good or evil, than there is in our classifying of objects as falling under different categories. For mistakes in our classifications of objects might make us foolish, but mistakes in our classifications of possible courses of action make us evil. And it is certainly more reprehensible to be evil than it is to be foolish.

But in the existentialist's ambiguous, indeterminate world, actions are not univocally good or evil; there are no unambiguous principles determining the ethical character of actions, just as there are no unambiguous principles determining the identities of objects. This apparently undermines the very foundations of morality because it seems that no action would be any more good than it is evil, or, otherwise stated, every action would be just as much good as it is evil. If this is the case, then the possibility of ethical judgment is put in jeopardy because, without any univocal ethical principles to determine the ethical character of an action, there seem to be no standards by which to judge actions as good or evil. But then we have no grounds on which to praise the actions of, say, Gandhi or Martin Luther King Jr., nor do we have grounds on which to condemn the actions of, say, Adolf Hitler or Harry Harlow. Standing up for the civil rights of the oppressed is, morally speaking, no different than committing genocide or torturing infants, and so, the type of life that we choose to lead makes no moral difference. This is clearly an untenable position because it reduces human life to an amoral free-for-all in which anything is permitted. But do existentialist philosophers have a way out of this predicament?

To gain a firmer foothold in the problem of an existentialist ethics, we need to take a closer look at the general problem of ethical judgment, which is in turn facilitated by examining the way in which philosophers have typically conceived of the foundation of such judgment. Taking their cue from Plato, most ethical theorists have derived the ethical character of actions from the relation between actions and human nature, or the human essence. Specifically, an action possesses a positive ethical character, or is good, if it advances the self-achievement of the person performing the action, whereas an action possesses a negative ethical character, or is evil, if it detracts from the self-achievement of the agent. And the shape of such self-achievement is defined by the human being's essence. For example, Plato conceives of the human being as essentially rational; the human being is defined by its possession of reason. Therefore, the human being approaches self-achievement to the extent that it acts rationally, to the extent that reason guides its behavior. For Plato, then, actions guided by reason are good, but irrational actions are evil. To cite another example, John Stuart Mill conceives of the human being as that which pursues the greatest happiness for the greatest number. Therefore, the human being approaches self-achievement to the extent that its actions are conducive to the greatest happiness. For Mill, then, actions conducive to the greatest happiness are good, and actions detrimental thereto are evil.

Notice that because ethical theories typically derive the ethical character of an action from the human essence, such theories will possess determinate, univocal standards for ethical judgment as long as they conceive of the human being as possessing a determinate, univocal essence—the essence is itself the standard for such judgment. However, existentialist ontologies conceive of the human being as essentially indeterminate. Because of the human being's fundamentally indeterminate structure, humans lack a univocal essence, and so the standard for judging the ethical character of human action is rendered indeterminate. On this basis, existentialism's problems, discussed earlier, regarding the ethical character of actions, and for ethically judging actions, quickly surface. If there is no determinate human essence, then there can be no univocal conception of what, exactly, it is for a human being to achieve itself. But then there can be no univocal standard to determine whether an action is good or evil. In other words, if there is nothing to determine whether an action advances or detracts from the self-achievement of the agent in question, then no action is any more good than it is evil. The question, again, is whether existentialism can escape this predicament. Or, does the existentialist's denial of a determinate human essence destroy the possibility of morality?

II. NIETZSCHE'S ETHICS—THE AMORALITY OF EXISTENCE

To understand the ethical dimension of Friedrich Nietzsche's thought, we must recall how he views the basic structure of all that exists, that is, as will to power, whose structure is unfulfillable self-transcendence. The unfulfillability of will to power renders it ambiguous; and although it does have a goal toward which it strives, its having a goal does not give it a univocal conceptual identity because that goal is indeterminate. This is the structure of all that exists, so for Nietzsche, both the human being and the world that it inhabits are will to power—unfulfillable, ambiguous self-transcendence; both are in a state of continual self-transformation in view of an indeterminate goal. And Nietzsche maintains that whatever is so structured is not subject to moral rules, or, as he puts it, is beyond good and evil.

The amoral character of the Nietzschean world can be seen in the following way. We have seen that philosophers typically base the ascription of ethical character on the extent to which a person's behavior advances or detracts from their pursuit of the goal of self-achievement, and that the human agent can only possess such a goal if it has a determinate structure in the form of an essence. If the human being lacks a determinate structure, lacks a univocal essence, then its behavior is not subject to ethical judgment; it is fundamentally amoral. Nietzsche extends this model of ethical character to include not only humans but the world as well. That is, an ambiguously structured world, just like an ambiguously structured human being, is impervious to ethical judgment: beyond good and evil. To attain a clearer conception of the amoral character of the Nietzschean world, it will be helpful to first examine how Platonic rationalism yields a *moral* world. For Nietzsche sees his own claim that the world is amoral as an essential point of contrast between his own worldview and that of the Platonic rationalist. And an understanding of the amorality of the Nietzschean world will facilitate our transition from Nietzsche's ontology to his ethics.

Previously, we cited the teleological and mechanistic worldviews as examples of rationalist worldviews, that is, of worldviews that posited unambiguous, determinate world-constituting, or world-structuring principles. For the purpose of understanding Nietzsche's conception of a moral worldview, we begin with the former. Recall that the teleological worldview understands events in the world to be driven by the world's pursuit of an ultimate, determinate goal. In addition, the teleologist sees this goal as giving the world its univocal conceptual identity because the world's various states are defined by their relation to the world's goal. Thus, as fundamental world-structuring principle, the goal toward which the world strives plays the role of an essence—it makes the world what it is, that is, that which pursues the goal in question. And so, this goal is the standard determining what it would be for the world to have attained self-achievement. That is, the world would be fully achieved if it were to instantiate the state-of-affairs adumbrated by its ultimate goal. There-fore, for the teleologist, the world approaches self-achievement to the extent that its states approximate its ultimate goal.

Thus, the teleological worldview sets forth a world-structuring principle that serves as a standard by which the world's various states can be judged. States-of-affairs that approximate the world's ultimate goal, that are conducive to the world's attaining self-achievement, are judged positively, whereas those that are detrimental thereto are judged negatively; in other words, states of the former type are good, whereas those of the latter type are evil. To illustrate, if a teleologist were to hold that the world pursues a state in which its inhabitants would be happy, then a rainstorm that facilitates crop growth would be judged as good weather, but a drought that destroys crops would be judged as bad weather. This is why, according to Nietzsche, the teleological worldview is a moral worldview; by positing a world-structuring principle that functions as a determinate essence, and thus as a determinate standard for judging the world's self-achievement, it sees the world as subject to ethical judgment.

Here, it might be objected that the teleologist's judgments concerning the world's instantiating good and bad states need not be, and typically are not, *ethical* judgments at all. After all, when one speaks of, say, good or bad weather, one is not praising or condemning the world morally, but in some other sense. Such judgments might be better seen as praising or condemning the world insofar as its weather states are convenient or inconvenient, not morally good or evil. Whether such judgments are actually based on convenience and inconvenience or some other set of alternatives, it seems clear that they should be taken in an amoral sense. Thus, it seems that Nietzsche's characterization of the teleological worldview as a moral worldview is mistaken. To this objection, the Nietzschean reply would be along the following lines. Although it may seem that the teleological worldview's ostensibly ethical judgments about the world's states are not really ethical, they actually are. For to believe that there is some final state of fulfillment, some ideal, perfect state of the world that is yet to be achieved, is to devalue the world as it actually is. It is to view the world as fundamentally lacking in worth—the world, as it is, is not as it *ought* to be. And to claim that something is not as it ought to be is to judge it ethically; it is to make a moral claim.

The teleologist's judgments concerning the world's states, then, are, according to Nietzsche, ethical judgments. Therefore, the teleological worldview is a moral worldview insofar as it permits the world to be judged ethically. Moreover, Nietzsche holds that all rationalist worldviews are moral worldviews. For what makes the teleological worldview a moral worldview is its positing of a determinate world-structuring principle, which is taken as a standard for judging the world's self-achievement. And all rationalist worldviews, teleological or not, posit such principles. To illustrate this, we consider some non-teleological rationalist ontologies.

The mechanistic worldview, as we have seen, is a rationalist worldview because it posits laws of nature as the determinate world-structuring principles that give the world its univocal conceptual identity. Things and events in the world are driven by their obedience to laws of cause and effect, and thus have their identities determined by their place within the chain of causes and effects. That is, the mechanist sees the system of natural causal laws as giving the world its univocal conceptual identity because the world's various states are defined by their place within this system of laws. As definitive of the world's univocal identity, the laws of nature that control events in the world play the role of an essence, that is, the world's essence. And so, the system of natural causal laws is the standard determining what it would be for the world to have attained self-achievement. Specifically, the world's self-achievement would be attained if it were to instantiate the state of affairs adumbrated by the laws of nature, the state-of-affairs in which these laws completely control the world's behavior.

Like the teleologist, the mechanist sets forth a world-structuring principle that serves as a standard by which the world's various states can be judged. In the former case, that standard is the ultimate goal that drives and defines the world's states, but in the latter case, the system of natural laws drives and defines the world's states. Therefore, for the teleologist, states of affairs are judged positively if they approximate the world's ultimate goal, and they are judged negatively if they fail to do so; whereas for the mechanist, states of affairs are judged positively if they approximate a world controlled by causal laws of nature, and they are judged negatively if they fail to do so. For instance, the mechanist would see events that obey the law of gravity as good; a world in which unsupported objects always fall is good because it functions as it ought to. On the other hand, if the law of gravity failed to obtain in some cases, the mechanist would see such occurrences as bad; a world in which unsupported objects sometimes float in the air is not functioning as it ought to. Thus, mechanists, like teleologists, judge the world's states to be good or evil; they judge the world ethically.

Here, as in the case of the teleologist, it seems at first that the mechanist is not really making ethical judgments when praising or condemning states of affairs. The reason for this appearance, however, is somewhat different in the mechanist's case. To see this, recall that, at first, the judgments of the teleologist did not seem to be ethical, but instead seemed to be amoral in some unspecified sense, perhaps as judgments concerning convenience. Still, we saw that the Nietzschean can reply that to praise an unachieved state of the world as better than the state that the world has already attained is, precisely, to make a moral judgment, insofar as the claim that the world is not as it ought to be is implicit in this judgment of praise.

Now, in the present case, the Nietzschean position that the mechanist's condemnation of a world that is not controlled by natural laws of cause and effect is a moral condemnation, and that the mechanist's praise of a world governed by such laws is moral praise, seems to be inaccurate for a different reason. That is, whereas it at least makes sense for a teleologist to make judgments concerning the world's moving in a better or worse direction—judgments that Nietzsche insists are, by their nature, ethical; it appears that the mechanist could have no occasion on which to make ethical judgments about the state of the world. For, from the teleologist's point of view, the world could either progress or deteriorate because there are no necessary laws forcing it to do one or the other—it could rain, but then again there could be a drought. But the mechanist's causal laws are necessary, unbreakable laws; according to the mechanist, events in the world will always be controlled by laws of cause and effect, and they always have been. So, if mechanists were to judge the world ethically, their judgments could only be positive. It hardly makes sense, then, to say that mechanists judge the world ethically. For if all judgments about something are necessarily positive, then such judgments are really no more than statements about what is in fact the case, not about what ought to be the case, and so they are not *ethical* judgments at all. It seems, then, that Nietzsche's characterization of the mechanistic worldview as a moral worldview is mistaken.

To counter this objection, Nietzsche would have to maintain that although mechanists could only judge the world positively, this does not prevent their judgments from being ethical, that there are still statements about what ought to be, and not just statements of fact, embedded in their judgments about the world. Here, we can make an argument on Nietzsche's behalf, showing that although, for the mechanist, it is impossible for there to be a negative state of affairs, and thus negative ethical judgments about the world are impossible, this does not strip the mechanist's judgments of their ethical character. This can be shown through the following examples.

Suppose I were to judge that triangles have three sides. This judgment is necessarily true because its negation is self-contradictory; being a triangle simply means having three sides. The necessary truth of the judgment reflects the fact that triangles could not be otherwise insofar as there would have to be non-three-sided three-sided figures for triangles to fail to be three-sided. In other words, the state of affairs that triangles have three sides could not be otherwise. To this extent, our judgment about triangles mirrors the mechanist's judgments about the world's obeying the causal laws of nature, for instance, the judgment that unsupported objects fall. In both cases, the judgments are necessarily affirmative because they are judgments concerning states of affairs that the mechanist would claim could not be otherwise. The question is this: Does the fact that both judgments can only be positive imply that they are simply statements of fact, of how things are, without an implicit judgment about how things ought to be?

Here, we must note a salient difference between the judgment about triangles and that about unsupported objects. In both cases, their falsity is impossible, but for different reasons. The judgment that all triangles have three sides cannot be false because the state of affairs that would make its negation true is *in principle* impossible; whereas the judgment that all unsupported objects fall cannot be false because the state of affairs that would make its negation true is impossible not in principle, but only in fact. That is, no possible state of affairs could count as triangles not having three sides; moreover, such a state of affairs would be self-contradictory, and self-contradictions are impossible both in fact and in principle. However, although, according to the mechanist, the laws of nature necessarily prevent unsupported objects from, say, floating, and so no possible state of affairs could count as unsupported objects not falling, nevertheless such a state of affairs is at least conceivable. For the idea of unsupported objects not falling can easily be imagined because it is not self-contradictory. Therefore, for the mechanist, the state of affairs that would make the negation of the judgment about unsupported objects true is impossible in fact, but is possible in principle.

But how does this distinction between judgments whose falsity would require the occurrence of a self-contradictory state of affairs, which is impossible in principle, and those whose falsity would require the occurrence of a state of affairs that is impossible in fact, but is not self-contradictory, affect the ethical character of those judgments? To answer this question, consider first the former type of judgment, that is, the judgment that triangles have three sides. As we have seen, for this judgment to be false, there would have to be a non–three-sided triangle, that is, a non–three-sided three-sided figure. But such a figure is impossible because its non–three-sidedness and its three-sidedness cancel each other out, leaving nothing at all. That is, the self-contradictory nature of the figure renders it impossible, and, furthermore, reduces it to nothing. To generalize the point, self-contradictory states of affairs are impossible because they are nothing at all; in other words, to say that a state of affairs is impossible in principle is to say that it is nothing. And this is why judgments whose falsity would require such a state of affairs have no ethical dimension. That is, to judge that something ought to be the case, there must be some state of affairs that ought not be the case; judging that something should be only makes sense if there is something opposed to it that should not be. Otherwise, the judgment is simply a judgment about what the case is, a statement of fact, and no more. Therefore, if all of the mechanist's judgments about the world were of this type, if they were judgments that could only be positive because their falsity required the occurrence of a self-contradictory state of affairs, then they could not be legitimately construed as ethical judgments, and so Nietzsche's characterization of the mechanistic worldview as a moral worldview would be mistaken.

However, as was pointed out earlier, although the mechanists's judgments about the world are always positive, they are typically judgments about states of affairs that could not be otherwise not because their falsity requires the occurrence of a self-contradictory state of affairs, but because the allegedly necessary laws of cause and effect control the world's behavior. And, as we have seen, violations of such laws are not self-contradictory, but are at least conceivable; we can perfectly well conceive, say, unsupported objects floating. Therefore, the mechanist's positive judgments concerning the world's obedience to natural laws of cause and effect are not simply statements of fact and no more, as are judgments whose falsity requires the occurrence of a self-contradiction. Rather, they harbor a moral claim, just as the judgments of the teleologist do because the states of affairs required for the mechanist's judgments to be false may be impossible, but they are not reduced to nothing; they are not impossible in principle. Thus, although such a state of affairs may, according to the mechanist, be impossible, it is *something*—specifically, something that ought not to be. The mechanist's judgments about the world are, then, ethical judgments, and so the mechanistic worldview is a moral worldview. Insofar as it posits a determinate world-structuring principle that is taken as a standard for judging the world's self-achievement, that is, insofar as it is a rationalist worldview, it permits the world to be judged ethically.

As a final illustration of a rationalist, and thus moral, worldview, we turn to the founder of rationalism: Plato himself. The sense in which Plato's worldview is moral can be seen by recalling the distinction that lies at the heart of his ontology—the distinction between Forms, or intelligible objects, and their instances, or sensible objects. Plato's Forms, as we have seen, make things the types of things that they are. They are the determinate, fundamental world-structuring principles that give sensible objects their univocal conceptual identities; they are the essences of things. And Plato prioritizes Forms over their instances by maintaining that sensible objects are deficient facsimiles of their respective Forms. Beset with accidental properties that introduce ambiguity into them, sensible objects are not fully achieved phenomena because it is the purely determinate Forms, which sensible objects emulate, that embody the true nature of such objects. For Plato, then, the true character of the world is its unambiguous Form-determined nature, and the world would attain self-achievement if it could rid itself of its accidental, ambiguous aspects, thereby becoming identical to the intelligible realm of the Forms.

Plato's worldview is clearly moral in the Nietzschean sense. Like the teleologist's ultimate goal and the mechanist's laws of cause and effect, the Platonic Forms give the world its determinate structure and serve as standards for judging the world. And these judgments are ethical in that the ambiguities of sensible objects are seen as rendering them inferior to the Forms. In other words, according to Plato, the world is not as it ought to be.

We can now understand why Nietzsche sees rationalism as implying the moral worldview. As we have seen, Nietzsche's fundamental ontological claim is that the world is, in fact, indeterminate, or that the world's basic character is forged by an indeterminate structuring principle—that is will to power. The rationalist, on the other hand, maintains that the world's basic structuring principle is determinate, and that the world would achieve itself if it were to attain a state of such determinacy. And this positing of a univocal world-structuring principle harbors an ethical claim about the world insofar as the determinacy of that principle yields a standard in terms of which the world's states count as better or worse. By way of this standard, finally, these states can be judged as better or worse, as good or evil. Nietzsche's irrationalism, on the other hand, yields an amoral worldview. That is, as noted earlier, without an unambiguous world-structuring principle, whether that principle takes the form of the world's ultimate goal, the world's ultimate truth, or the system of rules by which the world functions, and thus without a univocal set of rules describing what it is for the world to be what it properly, or in truth, is, there is no determinate formula describing how the world ought to be. Like a work of art, then, the world is fashioned without any determinate set of rules by which its states could count as, and thus be judged as, better or worse. Hence, Nietzsche's claim that his worldview is amoral. The Nietzschean world as will is impervious to ethical judgment—beyond good and evil.

Thus far, we have seen how Nietzsche's existentialist ontology, his ontology of will to power, leads to an amoral worldview. This worldview's claim that the world is not subject to ethical judgment is not terribly controversial; most of us would agree that the world itself is neither good nor bad in any moral sense. However, Nietzsche views all of existence, including human beings, as will to power. Hence, human actions, according to Nietzsche, are as immune to ethical judgment as is the behavior of the world. Just as the world's lack of a determinate structuring principle, of a univocal essence, implies that its behavior is not subject to ethical judgment, so the human being's lack of a univocal essence renders human behavior beyond the scope of ethical judgment. And this claim is certainly controversial. For whereas most of us would agree that the behavior of the world is morally neither good nor bad, few, if any, of us would extend this amorality to the behavior of humans. As pointed out earlier, to do so apparently endorses a view of human life in which anything is permitted. Before jumping, in Nietzsche's name, to this unpalatable conclusion, we need to take a closer look at his analysis, and critique, of morality.

According to Nietzsche, morality arises from a human need, that is, the need to live in a community. This is why he characterizes all morality as "herd" morality, the morality of a community. The main-tenance of a community requires morality because a community cannot survive without consistency in the behavior of its members. That is, the unity and stability of a community can only be maintained if its members follow generally similar patterns of behavior. Otherwise, the community is reduced to a disconnected conglomeration of agents acting arbitrarily, without any connection among them except their spatial proximity to one another, and so the community disinte-grates. The maintenance of a community, then, requires rules or laws regulating our actions—moral laws. And such moral laws must be determinate, univocal, rational laws; thus, morality is necessarily a rationalist institution.

To see, more precisely, the rationalist character of morality, that is, why moral laws must be determinate, we must examine how the relation between moral laws and the human community is isomor-phic with the relation between the rationalist's determinate world-structuring principles and the world that such principles structure. Determinate world-structuring principles give objects their univocal identities, thereby giving them the stability to endure, to undergo change without losing those identities. Such principles give stability to objects by setting restrictions on the types of changes that they can undergo while maintaining their conceptual identities. Therefore, the determinate world-structuring principles that lie at the heart of Pla-tonic rationalism, whether they take the form of an ultimate goal, a system of causal laws, or Plato's world of ideal Forms, are rules or laws for the behavior of objects. They determine what objects may do while maintaining their univocal identities. Or what, in view of our analysis of the moral dimension of determinate world-structuring principles, amounts to the same thing: Such principles determine what it is for objects to be properly or improperly behaving, or how objects ought to behave. This, as we have seen, is why rationalist worldviews are necessarily moral worldviews. And as long as objects are obedient to these laws, the world is itself stable, consistent, predictable because objects will not violate the rules set forth by its ultimate structuring principles. Ultimately, then, a world whose objects and events follow the laws set down by determinate principles is an orderly world, a rational world.

We can now see the similarity between rules that guide the behavior of objects and rules that guide the behavior of human agents. (We will refer to the former as *natural* laws and the latter as *moral* laws, although, from Nietzsche's point of view, natural laws also possess a moral dimension.) Just as natural laws give objects their univocal identities, so moral laws allow human agents to forge such identities. That is, just as objects maintain their univocal identities by behaving in ways that are restricted by rules regarding the states that they can embody, by obeying natural laws, so human agents maintain their univocal identities by acting in accordance with moral laws. For instance, a chair cannot walk and talk without failing to be what it is, and so without losing its identity, because of laws determining the proper behavior of chairs. Similarly, human agents whose actions qualify as good, as those of properly behaving people, would, in a sense, no longer be the same people if they began acting in an evil manner, if they began behaving in a way that breached the laws determining the proper behavior of a human agent. To justify this last claim, we must determine the sense in which a person's behavior changing from good to evil would constitute a loss of their identity because it is not obvious that this is the case. After all, although chairs certainly cannot walk and talk while still being chairs, it seems that a good person can become evil and still be the same person.

Still, people who turn evil does lose their identity in an important sense, that is, their identity as a member of their community. For such people become detrimental to the survival of the community of which they are members because they violate the community's need for stability and consistency in the behavior of its members. The proliferation of such people would lead to the disintegration of the community.

Those who turn evil lose their identity within the community by being removed from it. In this way, just as natural laws give the objects that obey them the stability to endure, so moral laws do the same for human agents. Moral laws determine what it is for human agents to behave properly or improperly, or how humans ought to behave. And as long as we obey these laws, our community is stable, consistent, predictable. Ultimately, a community whose members follow determinate moral laws is an orderly, and thus a functioning, community—a rational community. Here, again, the rationalist character of morality is clear: the purpose of moral laws is to maintain a community, and the unity of a community requires that these laws be univocal, to engender consistency, or order, in the behavior of its members.

Through the previous analysis, we gain a clearer view of the human need from which, Nietzsche maintains, morality arises. The need to live in a community, which gives rise to the institution of morality, is a need for order and stability. And according to Nietzsche, this need for order and stability is the fundamental motivation behind any form of Platonic rationalism, whether it be the rationalist ontologist's assertion of univocal laws guiding the natural world, or the rationalist ethicist's assertion of univocal laws guiding the human community. Nietzsche's claim is that just as the former needs the behavior of objects and events to be stable and orderly, so the latter needs the behavior of human agents to be stable and orderly. With these parallels in mind, we can see that Nietzsche's critique of morality is essentially identical with his critique of Platonic rationalist ontology and the various forms that it takes, such as science. In either case, the rationalist misinterprets the fundamental character of existence—the rationalist makes the cognitive error of believing that the world is determinate, but it is actually indeterminate. But Nietzsche makes the further claim that the rationalist *needs* to so misinterpret the world, that there is more than a merely cognitive error underlying Platonic rationalism.

The question to be addressed now is this: Why, according to Nietzsche, does the rationalist need to misinterpret the world as determinate? Why does the rationalist need to believe that all existence is stable and orderly, that both human and nonhuman existence are guided by laws? Nietzsche's answer: because rationalists suffer from a form of weakness. This claim that the need for order, stability, consistency, is born of weakness can be understood in the following way.

Recall Nietzsche's conception of power. We have seen that will, for Nietzsche, is necessarily will to power because will, being self-transcendent, continually transforms itself, overcomes itself, becomes different than what it was. And such self-transformation is growth, which Nietzsche equates with power. Thus, to grow, to be powerful, is to be self-transforming. With this notion of power in mind, it follows that weakness is the inability to grow, to transform oneself. For Nietzsche, then, stability, or resistance to transformation, is a weakness.

We can now see the connection between Platonic rationalism and weakness. Stability or consistency, as we have seen, results from a thing's behavior being restricted by laws, that is, by its possession of a univocal, determinate identity. And the basic claim of Platonic rationalism is that the world and the things that populate it have such identities. Moreover, Nietzsche holds that rationalists need to interpret the world in this way because they cannot accept the world's true ambiguity—its unstable, inconsistent, self-transformative nature—and so they cover the world with an illusory veil of rationality. The rationality of this veil is then asserted to describe not only the world as it actually is, but as it ought to be as well. That is, determinacy or univocity are judged to be morally good, but indeterminacy is judged to be morally evil. This is why Nietzsche often claims that the rationalist's misinterpretation of the world exhibits a hatred of the world and of life. Unable to accept and cope with the world's true indeterminacy, the rationalist's need for order and stability causes him to lash out against existence, and to slander it as evil. Ultimately, Nietzsche maintains that this inability to cope with indeterminacy reflects the rationalist's inability to, himself, live unstably, inconsistently, self-transformatively. That is, it is a manifestation of the rationalist's inability to grow, to exercise power; so rationalist ontology is a manifestation of the rationalist ontologist's own weakness.

But how, exactly, is the rationalist's assertion of stability in objects, of the world's inability to exercise power, a sign of the rationalist's own weakness? This can be seen by looking to rationalist ethics, which is a clearer manifestation of this weakness. Although the rationalist ontologist maintains that objects ought to behave in a stable, consistent way, the rationalist ethicist maintains that human beings ought to act in this manner. And this valorization of a life of stability reveals the type of life that rationalists pursue, that is, a self-consistent life driven by determinate laws—a life that resists self-transformation, a life guided by weakness. Rationalists, then, lack the strength to live without determinate rules, to live inconsistently by continually transforming themselves into different people, to live amorally. Here, it might be objected that although Nietzsche characterizes the rational, moral life negatively, as a symptom of weakness, it is actually preferable to the

Nietzschean life of power. Before addressing this objection, it will be helpful to take a closer look at the type of life that Nietzsche endorses as the life of power.

Nietzsche refers to the person who lives the amoral life of power as the "overman." We can understand the nature of such a life by noting that Nietzsche characterizes it as powerful insofar as its structure is that of will to power. And, as we have seen, will to power is unfulfillable self-transcendence, constantly transforming itself because of its lack of a determinate goal. Will to power, then, is in a constant state of flux, devoid of a univocal identity. But what, exactly, would a life that is so structured amount to? At first glance, it might seem that such a life would be wildly incoherent. That the life of power lacks a determinate goal, and thus a univocal identity, seems to imply that the states embodied by the person living this type of life would be completely disconnected. Living without any univocal identity to restrict their behavior, without moral rules, it appears that the powerful act completely randomly, and so lack a coherent, enduring self. Ultimately, no course of action counts as better or worse, more or less preferable, good or evil because there is no enduring self to determine what is proper or improper behavior. Hence, Nietzsche's position is threatened by the problem, noted at the beginning of this chapter, that besets any existentialist ethics—the specter of human life being reduced to an amoral free-for-all.

To temper this picture of the life of the overman, we must recall that although will to power lacks a determinate goal, and so lacks a univocal identity, it is not completely devoid of an identity. Rather, will to power continually transforms itself in view of an ambiguous, indeterminate goal, thereby maintaining an ambiguous identity throughout its self-transformative career. The importance of this can be seen by recalling our analysis of Nietzsche's conception of the indeterminacy of objects. There, we saw that the indeterminacy of their identities implies that the various states that things can take on are as much instances of growth as they are instances of decay; these states are equally proper and improper. Things, then, conceived as will to power, inhabit a kind of ontological gray area—what, exactly, a thing is, what counts as proper or improper behavior for it, is ambiguous. As things transform themselves, they maintain an identity, but an ambiguous one; whether a thing is this type of thing or that, and thus whether its behavior is proper or improper, is never fully determined.

Applying, now, this analysis of will to power to the human being and its behavior, we can say the following. The human agent possesses an indeterminate identity, his actions are equally proper and improper. The human agent inhabits a *moral* gray area—who, exactly, a human being is, what counts as good or evil behavior, is ambiguous. As the human agent transforms himself, the human agent maintains an identity, but an ambiguous one; whether he is a good person or an evil person is never fully determined. And the implication of this is not that human life is an amoral free-for-all but, rather, that it is fraught with uncertainty. But how, exactly, are these two types of lives different? A person living a life of the first type would not be uncertain about the propriety of his actions because the question of propriety would have absolutely no purchase on the person's behavior. The person would behave recklessly, doing whatever he pleased, with the assurance that the character of his actions was ultimately inconsequential. This would be a life of radical permissiveness, opening the door to all manner of infamous behavior. The Nietzschean life of power, on the other hand, being beset with uncertainty, leaves the question of propriety always unanswered. This is why Nietzsche typically characterizes the life of the overman as one of courage and risk. Without determinate laws by which to determine good and evil, and thus without a way of definitively determining what one ought to do, the powerful nevertheless see that they must act, thereby constantly risking themselves, risking their identity, their being a person of a given type. To live in this way, to constantly transform oneself, pursuing various, ever-changing modes of behavior, experimenting with oneself, and all in the face of the uncertainty that arises when determinate moral rules are suspended, is to exercise power.

But the question remains: Why should we agree with Nietzsche's assertion that a life of risk, of self-transformation, in which one constantly re-fashions herself, is preferable to a life of stability, a consistent life, in which one establishes a determinate, univocal identity for oneself? The moral life, after all, does not suffer from the uncertainty of the amoral life; it follows articulable rules by which one can be assured that she is behaving properly. Nietzsche's answer is that the moral life is unnatural, a kind of degeneracy, a disease. That is, because the human being's basic ontological structure, its nature, is that of will to power, and because the amoral life reflects the self-transcendent structure of will to power whereas the moral life is in conflict with this structure, to live morally goes against the human being's fundamental nature.

Our analysis of Nietzsche's critique of morality allows us to understand some of Nietzsche's more infamous claims, most importantly, his valorization of power and his denigration of weakness. In this regard, Nietzsche is often taken to be endorsing the life epitomized by that of the fascist dictator. In fact, Germany's National Socialist leaders often cited Nietzsche as providing a philosophical justification for their actions. But, as we can now see, this is not the sort of power that the overman exercises. The power wielded by the overman is not the power to subdue others, but the power to resist the temptation of the moral life with its self-assured certainty; it is the power to continually change oneself despite the uncertainty inherent in the amoral, irrational life.

We can now also understand Nietzsche's notorious valorization of pain and suffering, which is best seen in relation to his equally notorious critique of pity and compassion. Nietzsche is critical of pity insofar as pity is felt for those who are in pain. To pity those who suffer presupposes that pain and suffering are evil, and that a good life is one devoid of suffering, a comfortable, painless life. However, pain is a necessary concomitant of change, of self-transformation because change is always destructive in that the establishment of a new state of affairs requires the destruction of the old one. Therefore, those who pity denigrate the self-transformative life, the life of power, in favor of a self-consistent, moral life. Pity, then, is a rationalist invention, a sign of weakness, and so Nietzsche valorizes pain and suffering because they are signs that one is changing, transforming oneself in accordance with one's nature as will to power.

Before concluding our exposition of Nietzsche's ethics, we take up one more possible objection to his position. Even if we grant that the amoral life is consonant with the human being's fundamental nature whereas the moral life is not, it could still be argued that the latter is preferable. For, as Nietzsche points out, our culture is one that endorses a life guided by rules designed to restrict our conduct, that strives for consistency and stability. And yet, our society is plagued by crime, violence, and strife. And those who bring these problems about are precisely those who refuse to regulate their conduct in accordance with the laws of morality. Thus, it seems that if moral prohibitions are abolished, as Nietzsche recommends, then our society would be plunged into an even worse situation, one in which the perpetrators of crime and violence, which is to say those who ignore the dictates of morality, are given free reign. With this in mind, it seems that what we need is not the abolition of morality but, rather, even stronger moral prohibitions than those that are already in place. Maybe allowing ourselves to live "naturally" would exacerbate rather than solve society's ills.

I believe that a Nietzschean response to this objection could take the following form. That the societal problems cited earlier exist can hardly be denied. But to infer from the existence of such problems that we need stronger prohibitions on our conduct, that we need more morality, more rules, rather than the abolition thereof, is not really justified. After all, our culture has lived under the yoke of morality at least since the time of Plato, and the result is the current plague of crime, violence, and strife that the defenders of morality are quick to point to as demanding stronger moral prohibitions. Seen in terms of its results, then, it seems that morality may very well be the problem. The Platonic rationalist's moral, rule-directed society has had more than two millennia to demonstrate its superiority over an amoral society, and has failed. Perhaps it is time to give the Nietzschean view of a society that encourages power a chance. This *might* very well have disastrous consequences, but we already *know* of the disastrous consequences that result from the imposition of moral rules. Morality, from the Nietzschean point of view, is a failed project; a new vision of humanity is called for—one that endorses the life of a human being who accepts the indeterminacy of all existence and who, therefore, embodies the values of power, courage, and risk, that is, the values of the self-transformative overman.

III. KIERKEGAARD'S ETHICS—THE RELIGIOUS LIFE

As we saw in our previous chapter, Søren Kierkegaard's primary concern was with the way to live a good, properly Christian, life. Thus, his thought focuses on questions regarding how one ought to behave—the subject matter of ethics. We also saw that Kierkegaard, like Nietzsche, conceives of the world as fundamentally indeterminate. However, Kierkegaard articulates this fundamental ambiguity not in terms of the world's self-transcendent character, as does Nietzsche but, rather, by focusing on the individuality of things, situations, and persons. Specifically, Kierkegaard maintains that the true character of things includes both their essential, or universal, properties, and their accidental, or individuating, properties, and that the individuating aspects of an object render it ambiguous. We have also seen that Kierkegaard claims that this worldview, which prioritizes the individual over the universal, is the true Christian worldview. Therefore, a properly Christian life is one that recognizes the individuality of all that exists, and thus accepts the world's fundamental indeterminacy. And because Kierkegaard's thought is concerned with how, exactly, to live such a life, the question that his thought addresses is, How does a person who accepts the world's indeterminacy behave?

To answer this question, we look to Kierkegaard's characterization of the three types of lives that a person can live. He names these lives the aesthetic life, the ethical life, and the religious life. The person living the aesthetic life aims solely at the satisfaction of his desires, and Kierkegaard claims that this is the lowest form of human life because the aesthete does not have a consistent, coherent self. That is, the aesthete's behavior lacks consistency because his actions, being driven by the pursuit of pleasure, must conform to, and thus change with, the contingencies of the situation in which the aesthete finds himself. For instance, if the specific desire that guided an aesthete's life were the desire for illegal drugs, then the aesthete would always do whatever it took to obtain them. But the courses of action that result in the acquisition of illegal drugs vary with one's circumstances. Contingent factors, such as the user's current financial resources, the current price of the drugs, the current availability of the drugs, and so on, would determine whether the drug user's behavior included, say, lying and stealing. If the drugs were inexpensive and readily available, then the user would not resort to lying and stealing, whereas scarcity of the drugs would result in his behaving in such an unseemly manner. Thus, that his behavior is guided by the pursuit of pleasure in the form of illegal drug use leaves the user without a consistent, coherent character.

Here, it should be noted that the drug user does have a coherent self in a sense, that is, he consistently pursues the acquisition of drugs. To generalize the point, the aesthete's behavior does not vary insofar as he is a pursuer of pleasure; aesthetes are consistently hedonists. Kierkegaard's characterization of the aesthete as lacking a coherent self, then, must be taken to mean that aesthetes lack a coherent *ethical* self; his actions lack *moral* consistency. In the case of drug users, he may or may not lie and steal, depending on the situation in which he finds himself. He may act morally or immorally, depending on his circumstances. And this moral variability is characteristic of anyone who leads an aesthetic life, regardless of what the aesthete takes as his specific life-guiding object of desire.

The person who leads the ethical life, however, possesses an ethically coherent self, and thus leads a higher type of life than does the aesthete. The ethical person acquires a coherent self because to live ethically, according to Kierkegaard, is to determine one's actions not in accordance with the pursuit of pleasure, but in accordance with moral laws. And such laws determine the moral character of an action, that an action is good or evil, regardless of the circumstances in which the agent finds herself. For example, to say that torture is morally wrong, that it violates the laws of morality, is to say that one should never perform acts of torture under any circumstances. The ethical person, then, always acts in accordance with the dictates of morality, and so her actions exhibit a moral consistency that the aesthete's actions do not exhibit. In this way, the person leading an ethical life gains a coherent self; her actions do not vary with the contingencies of the situation in which she finds herself. Hence, although the aesthete lives an inconsistent life guided by the pursuit of pleasure, the ethical person lives a consistent life guided by the demands of moral duty.

The difference between the aesthetic and ethical lives can now be articulated in terms of the distinction that, as we have seen, lies at the heart of Kierkegaard's thought, that is, the distinction between the individual and the universal. Recall that the universal character of a thing refers to that which makes it the type of thing that it is, and so is possessed universally by things of that type. In other words, the universal character of a thing is found in its essential properties. However, the individual character of a thing includes that which is irrelevant to its being the type of thing that it is, that which distinguishes it from other things of its type, distinguishes it as this particular thing of that type, and so is not possessed universally by things of that type. In other words, the individual character of a thing includes its accidental properties. Recall also that the universal character of a thing lends determinacy to that thing because its essential properties make it a determinate type of thing, whereas the individual character of a thing renders it ambiguous. As we had put it in our previous chapter, a thing's essential properties, determining it to be an X, are its X properties, whereas its accidental properties, being irrelevant to its being an X, are its non-X properties. An ontology that prioritizes the universal, then, equates the true character of a thing with its universal character—things are, in truth, determinate, univocal, rational. An ontology that prioritizes the individual, on the other hand, equates the true character of a thing with its individual character—things are, in truth, indeterminate, ambiguous, irrational. And this prioritization is the foundation of Kierkegaard's irrationalist, existentialist ontology, but the prioritization of the universal is the foundation of the ontology of Platonic rationalism.

Returning now to the difference between the aesthetic and ethical lives, notice that the ethical life prioritizes the universal. That is, the ethical person determines how to behave in a given situation by ignoring the contingencies of that situation. This can be clarified with an example. Suppose that a relative of mine is suffering from a mildly painful, curable disease, and is being kept alive by a life support system. Suppose, further, that this relative has asked me to take him off life support so he can die. Suppose, finally, that the laws of morality determine that ending an innocent life is tantamount to an act of murder, and that murder is morally evil. Should I honor his request? If I were leading an ethical life, I would not do so, for the following reasons.

If ending an innocent life is equivalent to murder, then the act of ending an innocent life meets all of the conditions required to classify an act as one of murder. In other words, it possesses all of the essential properties that make murders count as murders. If I were an ethical person, the fact that the act requested by my relative possesses these properties is all that I would need to consider in deciding whether or not to honor his request because they determine the act to be evil, regardless of the circumstances, regardless of the contingent, individuating aspects of the situation. Thus, if I were to act ethically, I would ignore the fact that my relative asked me to remove his life support, as well as the fact that he is in some pain. These facts are merely accidental to the true moral character of the act of removing life support; they would individuate the act of life support removal as being this particular act of life support removal, but they are irrelevant to the murderous, and thus evil, character thereof. That is, the ethical person treats the situation, and therefore the act performed within that situation, strictly in terms of its universal aspect, and thus in accordance with a rationalist ontology. Ignoring the contingencies of the situation, I would view the removal of life support in its univocal, determinate character, that is, as a case of murder. Therefore, even if the contingencies of the situation were different, say, if my relative's disease were excruciatingly painful as well as incurable, I would still refuse to take him off of life support. For the removal of life support, being the ending of an innocent life, would still possess the essential murder properties. This is how the ethical person's prioritization of the universal results in his actions being consistent—if the termination of an innocent life is morally evil, then he would never remove life support, no matter what the circumstances might be.

In contrast with the ethical person's prioritization of the universal, the person leading the aesthetic life prioritizes the individual. For, as we have seen, the aesthete's actions are driven by her pursuit of pleasure, and so they vary in accordance with the contingencies of the circumstances. In being driven by the pursuit of pleasure, the aesthete's behavior is guided by her circumstances. This amounts to a prioritization of the individual insofar as the contingencies of the situation in which one finds oneself, that is, the accidental properties of the situation, are precisely the individuating aspects thereof. The aesthete regards situations, and, therefore, the actions performed within these situations, in terms of their individuating aspects.

But if this is the aesthete's view of the world, then a question immediately arises: Is the aesthete the person who accepts the indeterminacy of existence? Is Kierkegaard's conception of a properly Christian life equivalent to the aesthetic life? Our description of the aesthetic life, as contrasted with the ethical life, may seem to suggest that this is, in fact, the case. For the life that Kierkegaard endorses is one that accepts the indeterminacy of the world in the sense that the person leading such a life views the true character of things and situations as including both their essential and accidental properties. To so view the world is to accept its indeterminacy insofar as it is accidental properties, the contingencies of things and circumstances, that introduce ambiguity into the world. And this acceptance of indeterminacy is, precisely, what distinguishes the aesthetic worldview from the ethical worldview, that is, from the worldview of the rationalist. Still, Kierkegaard prioritizes the ethical life over the aesthetic life. To understand why this is the case, we must take a closer look at the life of the aesthete.

Returning to our example of the relative who requests that I remove his life support, if I were an aesthete faced with this situation, my course of action would be determined by the amount of pleasure or pain that it would bring to me. For example, if I were not particularly fond of this relative, and I also knew that I were the sole beneficiary of his life insurance policy, I would be inclined to honor his request. I would also be so inclined if I would sorely miss him were he to die, but also believed that my grief would be overcome by my love of money. On the other hand, I would not be inclined to remove his life support if I believed that I would be sent to prison for doing so.

The point to notice, here, is that ethical considerations do not enter into the aesthete's deliberations. Therefore, his view of situations and of actions performed within those situations differs from the view of the ethical person, insofar as the latter sees situations and actions as ethically univocal, as unambiguously good or evil, but the aesthete does not. Yet, aesthetes do not view situations and actions as ethically ambiguous either. Instead, he completely overlooks the ethical dimension; situations and actions, for the aesthete, are not ethically ambiguous but, rather, are simply devoid of ethical implications. The aesthetic life, then, is not born of an existentialist worldview, a worldview that sees human actions as amoral because of their moral indeterminacy. Instead, the aesthetic life is similar to the amoral free-for-all that Nietzsche often seems to endorse, although, as we have seen, does not endorse, that is, a life in which the question concerning the propriety of one's actions has absolutely no purchase on one's behavior. Neither Kierkegaard nor Nietzsche countenances such a life.

We are now prepared to examine the sort of life that Kierkegaard's existentialist principles do endorse—the properly Christian, or religious, life. As Kierkegaard conceives it, the religious life exhibits important similarities with the aesthetic and ethical lives. Recognizing the indeterminacy of existence, the religious person, like the aesthete, prioritizes the individual over the universal, resulting in an inconsistent life insofar as the religious person's actions vary with the contingencies of the situations in which she finds herself. More specifically, both the aesthete and the religious person lead lives that are inconsistent with regard to the ethical character of their actions. That is, the religious person's actions, like those of the aesthete, are not consistently in accordance with the dictates of moral law. Just as the aesthete may act immorally, as in the case of the drug user who steals when he cannot afford to buy his drugs, so the religious person's way of life may lead to immoral actions. For both the aesthete and the religious person take the individual character of their circumstances into account when determining how to act, rather than seeing the situation solely in terms of its ethically universal character; they both prioritize the individual. In view of its similarities with the aesthetic life, Kierkegaard seems to have a rather curious notion of the religious life. Particularly, it seems strange to say that a truly religious life leaves room for immorality. Granted, people often invoke religious convictions to defend their immoral courses of action, but such invocations are typically taken as evidence that such people are not true practitioners of their professed religion. With this apparent problem in mind, we take a closer look at Kierkegaard's religious life.

Although the religious life's prioritization of the individual parallels the aesthetic life's prioritization thereof, in both cases leaving open the possibility of immoral action, the former differs from the latter insofar as the religious person acknowledges the legitimacy of universal ethical law. That is, whereas ethical considerations do not enter into the aesthete's deliberations regarding how to behave, the religious person does take the demands of morality into account; situations and actions, for the religious person, are far from being devoid of ethical implications. And herein lies the similarity between the religious and ethical lives. Both recognize the universal legitimacy of moral law; both recognize that actions are good or evil regardless of the circumstances within which they might be carried out.

Notice the apparent incoherence of Kierkegaard's characterization of the religious life. The religious person prioritizes the individual, allowing the contingencies of his circumstances to determine his behavior. At the same time, however, he acknowledges the legitimacy of ethical law. But to do this is, apparently, to prioritize the universal because ethical law is, by its very nature, universal. That is, it would be self-contradictory to recognize the legitimacy of ethical law and still allow individuating circumstances to play any role in determining one's actions. For to accept moral law is to maintain that one must act in accordance with it *regardless* of the particular situation in which one finds oneself. Is, then, Kierkegaard's religious life no more than a self-contradiction, and therefore impossible? Kierkegaard's answer: The religious life is, indeed, paradoxical, but it is not impossible to lead such a paradoxical life. To understand the precise nature of this life, we must further explicate the difference between the aesthetic prioritization of the individual and the religious prioritization thereof.

As we have seen, the aesthete's prioritization of the individual completely excludes any consideration of the universal; the contingencies of the situation determine the aesthete's behavior to the complete exclusion of the dictates of moral law because the aesthete does not recognize the legitimacy of the ethical. The religious prioritization of the individual, on the other hand, does not simply overlook the ethical dimension, but it still subordinates universal ethical law to individual circumstances; individuating circumstances hold priority over ethical demands. In this way, the legitimacy of moral law is acknowledged without prioritizing the universal. But how is this not tantamount to the aesthete's simple denial of ethical law? That is, if individuating circumstances can always outweigh ethical demands, then how does this amount to the legitimacy of moral law being acknowledged rather than simply denied?

In Kierkegaard's terms, the religious person does not deny ethical law, but suspends it when the exigencies of the circumstances in which he finds himself call for the breaching of moral rules. In such cases, ethical law is put out of play, overridden. Such a suspension of morality opens the door to religiously sanctioned immoral behavior, but the legitimacy of ethical law is not thereby denied. Admittedly, this sounds like little more than double-talk. For if the legitimacy of ethical law is accepted, it must be accepted as universal, as itself overriding the exigencies of any and every possible set of particular circumstances, because the universality of the ethical, its intolerance of exceptions, is essential to the very idea of ethical law, for Kierkegaard. The question is, What would a life that is caught in this tension between the prioritization of individuating circumstances and the legitimacy of universal moral law, a life caught in the paradox of the religious, amount to? Briefly put, it is a life of anxiety, a life of constant uncertainty. This can be seen by, again, contrasting the aesthetic and religious prioritizations of the individual.

The aesthete's prioritization of the individual simply denies the legitimacy of the universal, so the individuating aspects of his circumstances always determine his courses of action. Not acknowledging any behavior-determining role for ethical law, aesthete's behavior is necessarily driven by the exigencies of his particular situations. Alternatively, religious person's acceptance of universal ethical law implies that moral considerations are not necessarily overridden by particular circumstances, but her prioritization of the individual implies that the latter always could override the former. And, furthermore, this combination of an acceptance of the universal along with a prioritization of the individual leaves the religious person irremediably uncertain as to whether a given situation is one in which individuating circumstances do override the legitimate claims of morality. For the only way that one could attain such certainty would be if there were a determinate rule establishing when ethical law should be suspended in view of individuating circumstances. But to follow rules for one's behavior is, precisely, to prioritize the universal; it is to ignore individuating circumstances in favor of laws that do not admit exceptions—universal rules. Therefore, if the religious life were shaped by such rules, it would be no different than the ethical life.

So, the religious person does not possess the aesthete's certainty that individual circumstances always override ethical law, because to believe that this is the case is to simply deny that ethical law has any purchase on one's behavior. Nor does she possess a determinate rule by which to be certain that the circumstances in which she may currently find herself override ethical law. She never knows if the present circumstances demand the suspension of ethical law, although she does know that any and every set of circumstances may. Hence, the uncertainty and anxiety of the religious life.

In view of the preceding, we can understand the sense in which the religious person's acceptance of the world's indeterminacy besets her life with ethical indeterminacy. The uncertainty of the religious life follows from the fact that the religious person never knows when ethical law is to be suspended, whereas the ethical person is certain that ethical law is never to be suspended, and the aesthete is certain that it is always to be suspended. That is, for the ethical person, all situations fall within the legislative scope of ethical law, but, for the aesthete, all situations lie beyond the legislative scope of such law. But, for the religious person, all situations are *both* within *and* beyond the scope of ethical law because this scope is *both* universal *and* always subject to suspension. With this formulation of the paradoxical character of the religious life, the indeterminacy of such a life becomes clear, as can be seen through the following.

If a particular situation falls within the scope of ethical law, then it is not a situation that calls for the suspension thereof; it is not an exception to the rules of morality. Alternatively, if a particular situation lies beyond the scope of ethical law, then it calls for the suspension of ethical law; it is an exception to the rules of morality. Therefore, because a person leading a religious life regards all situations as both within and beyond the scope of ethical law, each situation, and thus the action performed within each situation, both is and is not an exception to the rules of morality. The religious person, then, can never be sure when circumstances call for the suspension of the rules of morality because each situation is indeterminate in this regard—the religious life is ethically indeterminate. All human actions inhabit the same ethical gray area of moral ambiguity that we saw to be characteristic of the Nietzschean life of will to power. That is, just as, for Nietzsche, the human agent's indeterminate identity, which follows from the indeterminacy of all existence, implies that all actions are equally proper and improper, and so the determination about what counts as good or evil behavior is rendered ambiguous; for Kierkegaard, the religious prioritization of the individual, which also follows from the indeterminacy of all existence, implies that any violation of ethical law is equally proper and improper, and so, again, the determination as to what counts as good or evil behavior is rendered ambiguous.

Here, a pivotal question, which was left unanswered in our analysis of Nietzsche's ethics, can be addressed: how, exactly, do agents faced with a morally indeterminate world determine their behavior? This question is particularly important because, as we have seen, it holds the key to resolving the basic problem of existentialist ethics—that such an ethics seems to imply that all courses of action are on equal moral footing. We have seen that this problem would disappear if there were a type of cognition that is geared to indeterminacy, a type of cognition that does not employ rigid formulas, but recognizes the ambiguity of existence, because such a mode of cognition would allow agents to determine the moral character of possible courses of action without the need for determinate moral principles. Within the context at hand, the question asks how Kierkegaard's religious person is able to determine when the particular, individual circumstances within which she must act override universal ethical law, even though there are no determinate, rational rules for making this determination. Can a familiar type of cognition serve as a model for, or at least clue to, the manner in which the religious person effects such judgments? Actually, we have already briefly characterized such a mode of cognition, that is, Platonic right opinion. We can see how right opinion constitutes such a cognitive mode by way of the following considerations.

Right opinion, as we have seen, is a vague, implicit grasp of what determines a thing to be the type of thing that it is. That is, it grasps the identities of things in an imprecise, inexact way, thereby regarding the world as ambiguous, indeterminate. The indeterminacy of this mode of cognition is most clearly seen when it is faced with objects that are not obviously a certain type of thing, objects that appear to be both X-like and non-X-like, such as beanbag chairs, which appear to be both chair-like and unchair-like. In the ethical realm, this indeterminacy comes to the fore in actions that appear to be both good and evil, such as euthanasia. The inexactitude that besets right opinion renders a life guided by this mode of cognition a life of uncertainty. For judgments made on the basis of right opinion are fallible. In the case of the beanbag chair, its appearing to be both chair-like and unchair-like leaves right opinion unable to determine, with infallible precision, whether or not it really is a chair. In the case of euthanasia, its appearing to be both good and evil leaves right opinion unable to determine, with infallible precision, whether or not it is the right thing to do.

Platonic right opinion, then, is a mode of cognition that is geared to indeterminacy, that acknowledges ambiguity; to this extent, it is the type of cognition that would allow us to make judgments about the character of things and actions in an ambiguous world. The question to be asked, now, is whether the ambiguity of the world as viewed by right opinion is equivalent to the ambiguity of the world as interpreted by Kierkegaard's ontology. If this is the case, then right opinion can serve as a model for the type of cognition that would allow Kierkegaard's religious person to make judgments about how she should act in a given situation, because both types of cognition would acknowledge, and thus be geared to, the same sort of indeterminacy. This would, in turn, give Kierkegaard an avenue for circumventing the accusation of lacking resources for making judgments regarding one's behavior.

To answer the question concerning the relation between the indeterminacy of the world of right opinion and that of the Kierkegaardian world, we must first note what it is that renders right opinion an ambiguous, and thus an uncertain, mode of cognition. From a Platonic point of view, the inexactitude of right opinion can be overcome by converting right opinion to knowledge, that is, by articulating the qualities that determine things to be the types of things that they are, and by using these formulas to judge the conceptual identities of things. As we saw earlier, this mode of cognition allows definitive determination of such identities, and so brings infallibility, and thus certainty, to our cognitive life—whether we are attempting to determine the conceptual identities of objects, such as beanbag chairs, or those of actions, such as euthanasia. In other words, knowledge overcomes the uncertainty of right opinion by focusing on the qualities that make X's X-like, in abstraction from those qualities that make those same things non-X-like. That is, knowledge views the world as determinate, by regarding things exclusively in terms of their essential properties, whereas right opinion sees the world as indeterminate, by regarding things insofar as they are composed of both essential properties (X properties) and accidental properties (non-X properties). Therefore, the uncertainty of the life of right opinion is a consequence of the fact that the objects proper to this mode of cognition, consisting of both X properties and non-X properties, both are and are not what they are; they are indeterminate, ambiguous, and so their identities can only be grasped inexactly.

Now we can see that the world as viewed by right opinion possesses the same sort of ambiguity as does Kierkegaard's world. That is, just as the former is ambiguous insofar as it is viewed as populated by things possessing both essential and accidental properties, both X properties and non-X properties; so Kierkegaard's world is ambiguous insofar as things are viewed as being, in their true character, individual. And, as we have seen, the individuality of things includes both their essential and their accidental properties. Individuals are indeterminate insofar as they are both X and non-X. With regard to the religious person's life of moral indeterminacy, the individuality of the situations within which the religious person acts renders them both exceptions to the rules of morality and not exceptions to the rules thereof—X and non-X. To determine whether or not to suspend ethical law, then, the religious person must use a type of cognition that is geared to such indeterminacy, a type of cognition that is guided by indeterminate standards in the same way that right opinion is so guided.

Therefore, Kierkegaard's denial of the ultimate propriety of a life guided by determinate principles, his subordination of the ethical life to the religious life, is not tantamount to a rejection of all standards by which to distinguish good from evil, and thus does not amount to an endorsement of a completely amoral free-for-all. Instead, the ambiguity of Kierkegaard's world still allows indeterminate standards for judgment, which can be grasped by an irrational mode of cognition, the mode of cognition employed by the religious person. And we can be sure that such modes of cognition are at least possible because, as we saw in our introductory chapter, most of our normal, everyday cognition, being guided by the indeterminate principles of right opinion, has precisely this character. This is not to say that the problem of Kierkegaard's version of an existentialist ethics has been fully resolved. A complete resolution would require a full analysis of the precise character of this indeterminate, inexact mode of cognition that allows the religious person to determine her actions, as well as an exhaustive characterization of the indeterminate standards that guide such cognition. This is a greater undertaking than can be attempted here. Still, we can now see that this would be no futile undertaking, as such a mode of cognition actually does exist, and we have seen that right opinion can serve as a model for explicating indeterminate cognition and the standards that guide it.

Notice that these considerations can also be invoked to give Nietzsche a way of avoiding the accusation that his ontology of will to power lacks resources for making judgments regarding how one should act. In Nietzsche's case, the relevant question is this: How does Nietzsche's overman determine when to exercise power, when to embark on a risky, courageous, self-transformative course of action? This is a problem because Nietzsche's overman, who lives a life that accords with the human being's fundamental ontological structure, that is, a life of power, is confronted with the same moral indeterminacy as is faced by Kierkegaard's religious person. In Nietzsche's case, the ambiguity of the world as will to power, as unfulfillable self-transcendence, renders the human being itself without a determinate identity, and thus with no univocal goal, or standard, by which to judge the propriety of its own actions. As we had put it in our discussion of Nietzsche's ontology, the goal toward which will to power strives is both G and not-G. Lacking an unambiguous standard, then, all of our actions are cases of both growth and decay; they bring us both closer to and further from the goal that measures the propriety of human action. Therefore, the Nietzschean overman, like Kierkegaard's religious person, can only determine the propriety of his actions by referring them to an indeterminate standard. And such a standard, as we have seen, can only be grasped through an indeterminate mode of cognition, specifically, a type of cognition whose basic structure is found in Platonic right opinion.

To complete our explication of Kierkegaard's conception of the religious life, we need to address a question that was mentioned earlier, that is, why does Kierkegaard refer to the life of moral indeterminacy as a, specifically, *religious* life? What do moral indeterminacy and religion have to do with each other? This can be answered by recalling that Kierkegaard sees Abraham as a paradigm example of a person leading a truly religious life. Abraham, Kierkegaard tells us, is the father of true Christian faith. Furthermore, Abraham's faith, his religious way of life, is most perspicuously illustrated in the Biblical story in which God commands him to kill his son, Isaac. And, according to Kierkegaard, this story reveals that Abraham lives a life of moral indeterminacy.

As Kierkegaard interprets the story of Abraham and Isaac, Abraham accepts the validity of universal ethical law; he acknowledges the ethical obligations that he has concerning his son. Still, when God tells him to sacrifice Isaac, he agrees to do so. From a Kierkegaardian point of view, Abraham's willingness to kill Isaac follows from his specifically religious prioritization of the individual. That is, though accepting the validity of the ethical law that forbids killing his son, he believes, nevertheless, that the individuating circumstances surrounding his intended murderous act, that is, that God commanded him to perform this act, will override the immorality of that act.

Here, it may seem as though Kierkegaard's endorsement of the religious life is a call to religious fanaticism because Abraham's justification for suspending ethical law is the fact that God commanded him to do so. This suggests that the religious person could invoke hearing the voice of God as justification for any sort of immoral behavior. That this is not Kierkegaard's position, however, can be seen by recalling that the person leading this type of life possesses no rules by which to determine when individuating circumstances override ethical law because living according to such rules would be equivalent to living an ethical, rather than a religious, life. Kierkegaard's religious person, then, cannot live by the rule saying that God's commands always override moral rules. Even if the religious person is commanded by God to act unethically, she can never be certain if this particular individuating circumstance calls for the suspension of morality.

In the final analysis, the religious life, for Kierkegaard, is one whose practitioners recognize the individuality, and thus the indeterminacy, of all that exists. This recognition, however, includes the acknowledgement of the legitimacy of universal law; hence, the paradoxical character of the religious life. This paradox—the simultaneous prioritization of the individual, combined with the acceptance of the legitimacy of the universal—saddles the religious person with constant moral uncertainty. Without ethical rules to follow, the religious person can never be sure about the propriety of her actions. The religious life, then, is a life of anxiety—an indeterminate life in an indeterminate world.

IV. HEIDEGGER'S ETHICS—THE INDETERMINACY OF DASEIN

The ethical dimension of Martin Heidegger's thought is particularly difficult to explicate because Heidegger explicitly denies that his thought possesses such a dimension; and, in keeping with this denial, he never developed an ethical theory. Nevertheless, one of the more pivotal notions in Heidegger's thought—that is, the notion of authenticity—concerns the type of life that is consistent with Dasein's basic ontological structure. In this sense, the life of authentic Dasein is the type of life that Dasein ought to live, and so Heidegger's conception of authenticity is akin to the traditional conception of ethical goodness; both concern the propriety of one's actions. With this in mind, we will, despite Heidegger's own cautions against doing so, articulate a Heideggerian ethics by focusing on his notion of authenticity.

Heidegger understands Dasein's authenticity in terms of its achieving wholeness. Here, the connection between Heideggerian authenticity and ethical goodness is patent because, as we have seen, philosophers have traditionally identified morally good actions as those that advance the self-achievement of the agent. A fully achieved human being, then, is an ethically good human being. And to be fully achieved is to attain wholeness; it is to be, wholly, what one properly is. Thus, to the extent that Heidegger equates Dasein's becoming authentic with its becoming whole, he sets his conception of authenticity squarely within the framework of traditional ethical philosophy. Authentic Dasein lives the type of life that it ought to in that it behaves in a way that renders it whole, in a way that is conducive to its self-achievement. However, for Heidegger, the very idea of self-achieved Dasein, of Dasein as having attained wholeness, is highly problematic.

The problematic character of Dasein's wholeness can be seen by recalling our discussion of Heidegger's ontology, particularly with regard to the impossibility of Dasein's achieving itself. This impossibility is rooted in the fundamental indeterminacy of the goal whose attainment would constitute Dasein's self-achievement. That is, Dasein strives toward gaining a full understanding of being, which would be tantamount to the overcoming of its passive dimension. This goal is indeterminate because Dasein's passive and active dimensions are equally essential to its ontological structure. For Dasein to achieve itself, then, it would have both to be and not be what it is— hence, the indeterminacy of its self-achievement. And this implies that Dasein's self-achievement is impossible. For if it were to lose its passive dimension, Dasein would no longer be Dasein. A fully achieved Dasein, then, is no Dasein at all.

Given the impossibility of Dasein's self-achievement, and the equivalence of Dasein's wholeness with its authenticity, the question that Heidegger must address asks whether authenticity is no more than a meaningless self-contradiction. Is an authentic life in any way possible? According to Heidegger, a proper understanding of authenticity, and of the way that it is possible, requires that we first understand the specific type of wholeness that is proper to Dasein. And Dasein's peculiar type of wholeness is understood through an examination of death.

Heidegger's examination of death notes that death is Dasein's end in two senses. Death is Dasein's end insofar as it is the point at which Dasein goes out of existence, the point at which Dasein comes to its end. At the same time, however, death is Dasein's end in the sense of being its goal. That is, death is that toward which all of Dasein's activities lead it; it is what Dasein continually moves toward. It is in view of these two senses in which death is Dasein's end, that Heidegger equates Dasein's death with its wholeness or self-achievement. For, as we have seen, Dasein's self-achievement, its overcoming of its passive dimension and thereby becoming a purely active object-constituting agent, is the ultimate purpose of all of its activities. In this sense, death and self-achievement play the same role for Dasein, that is, the role of Dasein's end in the sense of its goal. Moreover, death and self-achievement are both states that Dasein cannot possibly achieve. For, as we have seen, Dasein can never reach its goal of self-achievement because this would entail that Dasein overcome its passive dimension, which is essential to its fundamental structure; and so self-achieved Dasein would no longer be Dasein. For the same reason, Dasein cannot reach its own death. That is, when Dasein dies, it no longer is; more specifically, it is no longer Dasein. Hence, death and self-achievement are equivalent insofar as they both play the role of Dasein's end in the sense of a wholeness that is tantamount to extinction.

In view of the equivalence between Dasein's death and its self-achievement, we can now begin to understand how Heidegger conceives Dasein's peculiar type of wholeness. Dasein's attaining wholeness in the sense of eclipsing the end toward which it continually moves is impossible, so the wholeness that it can attain must be of a different sort. As Heidegger puts it, Dasein's end is such that it can never be *at* it, although it not only can be, but more precisely always is, *toward* it. That is, although Dasein can never reach its end, and so can never be at, or exist within, it, this end is its goal, and thus Dasein always directs itself toward it. We can now see that although authenticity cannot be equivalent to Dasein's arriving at its end, as so defining authenticity would render it impossible; authenticity also cannot be equivalent to Dasein's being directed toward, or striving after, its end, as this way of defining it would render authenticity unavoidable. Authenticity, then, must consist not simply in directing oneself toward one's end, but in doing so in a distinctive manner, in directing oneself toward one's own death, or self-achievement, in an appropriate way. In Heideggerian terms, Dasein attains wholeness through authentic being-toward-death.

The question to be addressed, now, concerns the appropriate way of being directed toward one's end, more specifically, toward an end that one necessarily pursues although it is in principle unattainable—an indeterminate goal. Heidegger refers to the state that Dasein attains when it is so directed as "resoluteness." To what is authentic Dasein resolved?—to the pursuit of its indeterminate, and thus unachievable, goal; to the fact that its self-achievement is its death. One of Heidegger's more incisive formulations of the nature of resoluteness occurs when he says that resolute Dasein conceives of its death as possibility. To do so is to maintain an "existential conception of death."

To view death as possibility is not to conceive it as a possibility that could be actualized. Rather, in keeping with the indeterminacy thereof, death is a possibility that must always remain merely possible and never actual. It is, in this specific sense, a pure possibility. And to view death as possibility is to view it as such a pure possibility. Here, it might be objected that an unactualizable possibility is really not possible at all, but is a mere impossibility, and so to characterize death as pure *possibility* is misleading. To better understand this objection, consider the following. Apparently, the relation that obtains between Dasein and its death is identical to that which obtains between Dasein and, say, its becoming a tree. For, in both cases, the relation is between Dasein and a state that Dasein cannot inhabit because Dasein would no longer be what it is. But, surely, one could not legitimately maintain that being a tree is a pure possibility for Dasein. Instead, it is simply impossible, a mere impossibility. Why, then, is this not true of Dasein's death? On what grounds does Heidegger maintain that death is a pure possibility, that is, impossible but nevertheless a possibility, rather than a mere impossibility?

The salient difference between these two cases, of course, is that although both are ways that Dasein would no longer be Dasein, and so are impossibilities, Dasein is not continually driven toward becoming a tree, but it is so driven toward its death because, as we have seen, its death is equivalent to its self-achievement. That is, although achieving itself in death is impossible for Dasein, it is peculiar among the many states that Dasein cannot possibly inhabit.

And death is peculiar in such a way that renders it more than a mere impossibility. As an impossible state toward which Dasein is necessarily drawn, death is an impossibility, but in the distinctive mode of an impossible *possibility*—a pure, because unachievable, possibility. And to be authentic, to live resolutely, is to recognize this, and to live accordingly.

But our question remains: What, exactly, is it to appropriately direct oneself toward one's indeterminate end, to live in a way that acknowledges this end as pure possibility? We approach this question by considering the criterion, or standard, by which the appropriateness of such directing of oneself is measured. Recall that Dasein's end is a pure possibility because of its indeterminacy; it is insofar as death, or self-achievement, is indeterminate that this end cannot be actualized, not simply in fact but in principle. And because Dasein's end is thus unactualizable, there is no univocal criterion by which to measure whether Dasein's actions advance or detract from its drive toward self-achievement. For the criterion that articulates an indeterminate goal must itself be indeterminate. Put in ethical terms, there is no determinate criterion by which to measure the ethical character of Dasein's actions—their advancing its drive toward self-achievement, and thus being good, or their detracting from its drive toward self-achievement, and thus being evil. Hence, Heidegger's subjection to the, now familiar, problem that besets existentialist ethics—the apparent lack of a standard by which to distinguish good and evil, by which to distinguish appropriate and inappropriate courses of action. Here, this apparent lack of a standard seems to imply that there is no appropriate way for Dasein to be directed toward its end because there seems to be nothing to distinguish the appropriate from the inappropriate.

But the lack of a determinate criterion for measuring the ethical quality of actions does not, as we have seen, necessarily imply a complete lack of standards by which to make such judgments. Kierkegaard's religious person and Nietzsche's overman employ irrational modes of cognition, pre-figured in Plato's notion of right opinion, to access specifically indeterminate standards for making such judgments. And the criterion in terms of which such judgments are effected is indeterminate because it articulates an indeterminate standard. In both cases, this indeterminacy does not render judgments concerning the propriety of one's actions impossible, but rather uncertain. This uncertainty lies at the heart of an existentialist ethics that is not reduced to mere permissiveness. But does Heidegger's version of an indeterminate criterion preclude such an untenable reduction, yielding instead a conception of ethical judgment as uncertain rather than simply meaningless?

Heidegger describes Dasein's indeterminate criterion of authenticity as a call to authenticity; Dasein is driven, and in this sense is *called*, to resolve itself to the pursuit of its unachievable goal. And because the call, being the criterion of authenticity, articulates an indeterminacy, it must itself be indeterminate. But, how, exactly, is the indeterminate to be expressed? Heidegger sees the call as articulating Dasein's indeterminate criterion with the expression "guilty." The connection between the indeterminacy of Dasein's end, articulated by the call, and guilt can be seen in the following way.

The call's accusation of guilt is directed at Dasein itself; it says that Dasein is the guilty party. Of what is Dasein guilty? Heidegger answers this question by explicating the basic nature of being guilty in general, which he maintains is being responsible for a lack. That is, to be guilty of something is to bear the responsibility for something negative, and the call accuses Dasein of bearing such a responsibility. It announces that Dasein is, in its very ontological structure, guilty in this sense. Specifically, the lack for which Dasein is responsible is its failure to attain self-achievement, to be fully actualized. This, primarily, is a lack insofar as self-achievement is that toward which Dasein is continually driven; it is the end whose actualization Dasein must pursue, but which must always remain uneclipsed. And Dasein is responsible for this lack because the unactualizability of its end is intrinsic to Dasein's very ontological structure. Dasein is always in an unachieved state, not because of the influence of some outside agency, but because of the fact that being deficient in this way is intrinsic to Dasein's way of existing. In this sense, Dasein bears the responsibility for its deficient state. This guilt is grounded in the indeterminacy of Dasein's end insofar as this indeterminacy renders Dasein deficient in its very ontological structure. It is, precisely, because the end to which Dasein is driven is indeterminate, and so is unachievable, that Dasein's self-achievement is impossible, a pure possibility. And herein lies the essence of Dasein's guilt.

In view of this, the call's pronouncement of Dasein's guilt is tantamount to a proclamation of the indeterminacy of Dasein's end. The call, then, articulates Dasein's indeterminate criterion of authenticity by proclaiming authenticity's indeterminacy. Unlike a determinate criterion, which, in this case, would offer a formula describing how Dasein must act to behave appropriately, authenticity's indeterminate criterion gives no specific rules for achieving authenticity, for properly being toward one's indeterminate end. Instead, it denies the possibility of such a univocal prescription. For Dasein's guilt is grounded in the indeterminacy of its end, and this indeterminacy precludes the criterion for authenticity from taking a determinate form. To be authentic, to be resolute, to be toward one's death, then, is to behave in a way that recognizes that the propriety of one's behavior cannot be univocally measured. That is, authenticity is achieved through a life of moral uncertainty. And, as in the cases of Nietzsche's overman and Kierkegaard's religious person, Heidegger's authentic Dasein is not left without any resources for making ethical judgments, despite the indeterminacy of the criterion by which such judgments are made. Like Kierkegaard's religious person and Nietzsche's overman, Heidegger's authentic Dasein is guided by an indeterminate criterion, rendering judgments regarding the propriety of one's actions uncertain, but not meaningless. The authentic life, then, is the life of uncertainty—an ethically ambiguous life that accords with the indeterminacy lying at the heart of Dasein's ontological structure.

V. SARTRE'S ETHICS—THE FREEDOM OF CONSCIOUSNESS

In our previous chapter, we saw that Jean-Paul Sartre's ontology admits the determinacy of nonhuman objects, while maintaining the indeterminacy of the human being, which seems to leave Sartre in a less radically irrationalist position than the other existentialists examined in our study. Although Nietzsche, Kierkegaard, and Heidegger view all existing things as indeterminate, Sartre attributes such ambiguity to the human being alone. However, the true radicality of Sartre's position comes to the fore in the ethical dimension of his thought. For the Sartrean version of the human being's indeterminacy gives rise to the basic problem of existentialist ethics in a particularly recalcitrant, if not irresolvable, way.

Our examination of Sartre's ethics begins by recalling his analysis of the human being's indeterminacy. This indeterminacy was seen to be a function of the human being's lack of an essence, a function of the emptiness of consciousness. For this emptiness leaves the human being without a univocal conceptual identity. That is, whatever content the human being does accrue is possessed by its ego; the ego's content consists of the characteristics that the human being accrues throughout the course of its existence. These properties make the human being a particular type of person. And because the ego is formed through the acts of empty consciousness, these acts are not beholden to any restrictions regarding the ego-content that they can construct, thereby rendering all ego-content intrinsically revisable. Thus, despite its accrual of ego-content, the human being remains without any essential, unrevisable determinations, without a univocal conceptual identity. In view of this, Sartre—like Nietzsche, Kierkegaard, and Heidegger before him—must confront the apparent implication that human life is an amoral free-for-all in which anything is permitted. And, as we have seen, Sartre's existentialist predecessors avoided this implication by conceiving of the standard for judging human action as ambiguous, rather than simply nonexistent. The question, then, is, Does Sartre's ontology of the human being allow for such a standard? To answer this question, we must take a closer look at the Sartrean version of the human being's indeterminacy.

Sartre's position is that the human being is indeterminate insofar as it is primarily identified with consciousness, which is devoid of all content. Now, if this empty consciousness were the entirety of the human being, then there would simply be no standard by which to judge human conduct; Sartre would have no way around the implication that all is permitted. This can be seen by way of the following. If the human being has no determinate identity, then there can be no determinate criterion by which to make ethical judgments. For, as we have seen, the existence of such a criterion requires the positing of a determinate human essence whose self-achievement plays the role of the standard for ethical judgment. Still, this does not preclude all ethical judgment. Even if the human being lacks a determinate identity, and so cannot be judged by a determinate criterion, it may possess an indeterminate, ambiguous identity, in which case its behavior could be judged in accordance with an indeterminate, ambiguous ethical standard. Thus conceiving of the human being as ambiguous, Nietzsche and Heidegger avoid the complete loss of ethical criteria. Notice, now, that if Sartre were to view the human being not only as primarily equivalent to empty consciousness, but as entirely equivalent thereto, then all ethical judgment would be rendered impossible. For empty consciousness is devoid of all content, and so has neither a determinate nor an indeterminate identity, leaving it with no standard, determinate or indeterminate, by which it can be judged. But the situation may not be so grave, for Sartre, because he does not maintain that consciousness makes up the entirety of the human being. Instead, the human being is primarily equivalent to consciousness, but the whole of the human being includes a secondary aspect—the ego. Does the human being's possession of an ego provide us with a criterion for ethical judgment?

At first, the human being's possession of an ego holds some promise for yielding a criterion by which its behavior can be judged. Although empty consciousness cannot be held to any ethical standard, determinate or indeterminate, because of its complete lack of content, the ego has content. The issue to be addressed is whether the content, the set of personal characteristics, possessed by the ego provides the human being with an ethical standard. With this in mind, we must examine the Sartrean ego with an eye to the precise sort of content it possesses.

Here, the key aspect of the ego's content is its revisability, which is the result of that content's originating in acts of empty consciousness. That is, because consciousness has no content, and thus no essential properties, nothing restricts the acts by which it constructs its ego. This, as we have seen, follows from the fact that a thing's essential properties, the characteristics that give it a univocal conceptual identity, are what restrict the thing's behavior. Lacking any properties at all, much less essential properties, consciousness is able to act in any arbitrary way, and thus to completely reconstruct its ego at any moment. Therefore, the content possessed by the ego can be completely revised at any point. The ego possesses content, but this content sets no restrictions on the future states that it can inhabit; nothing prevents the human being from making herself into a radically different type of person than she has been in the past. In the context of Sartre's ethical theory, this lack of restrictions on human action is the human being's freedom. Herein lies one of the basic tenets of Sartrean existentialism—the radical freedom of the human being.

The question that must now be addressed is, How does the revisability of the ego's content, which is rooted in the human being's freedom, affect the ego's ability to provide the human being with a criterion for ethical judgment? This is best approached by considering the extent to which the ego may or may not provide the human being with an identity.

Recall that no ethical standard is applicable to consciousness because consciousness has no content at all. Put in terms of its identity, consciousness, being devoid of content, lacks an identity, whether determinate or indeterminate. This lack of identity leaves consciousness without a self to be achieved, and thus without a standard for judging self-achievement, that is, without a standard for ethical judgment. The earlier question concerning the revisability of ego-content, then, can be restated as Does the ego have the sort of content that provides it with an identity? Or does the revisability of the ego's content leave it without an identity, and thus without an ethical criterion?

We have already seen that the revisibility of ego-content precludes the human being from possessing a determinate identity. For the possession thereof is equivalent to the possession of an essence because a thing's essence makes that thing, univocally, what it is. In other words, a thing's essential properties, in contrast to its accidental properties, make it a univocal X, rather than an ambiguous X and non-X. And, as we have also seen, it is the revisibility of ego-content that renders the ego unfit to provide the human being with essential properties, as such properties are, precisely, those that resist revision. Ego-content, then, is not the sort of content that gives its possessor a determinate identity, and so the human being's possession of an ego does not yield a determinate standard for judging its behavior. But does ego-content give the human being an indeterminate identity, and thus an indeterminate standard for ethical judgment? From the Sartrean point of view, it does not because the revisability of ego-content renders the ego unable to provide the human being with any identity at all, determinate or indeterminate. This can be understood in the following way.

As we have seen, the ego's revisability is rooted in its being the product of acts of empty, unrestricted consciousness. For this reason, the ego holds a merely secondary status; the human being is primarily equivalent to consciousness, whereas its ego is an aspect of the human being that is unilaterally dependent upon consciousness. Because of this dependence, and the unlimited malleability of the ego that it implies, ego-content is not definitive of the human being that possesses such content, and so does not give the human being an identity at all. This can be seen by returning to our example of my being a stingy person who suddenly becomes generous. In this case, my stinginess-content in no way defines me because it sets no restrictions on my present behavior. I may just as well have been consistently generous in the past, thereby constructing a generous, rather than a stingy, ego, and it would in no way have affected my ability to now be generous or stingy. The general point, here, is that the character of my ego does not affect how I behave; my ego-content does not determine the sort of person that I am—it does not give me an identity. Therefore, even though, for Sartre, empty, contentless consciousness is not the entirety of the human being, insofar as the entire human being includes its content-laden ego; nevertheless, the fact that ego-content is produced by acts of empty consciousness leaves the human being just as devoid of an identity, and thus of an ethical standard, as it would be if the human being were no more than mere empty consciousness. For, ultimately, Sartre's position is that not only does the human being lack a determinate, univocal identity, but it lacks any identity at all.

We can understand Sartre's well-known conception of "bad faith," which is a denial of one's own freedom, in terms of the human being's complete lack of an identity. More specifically, to live in bad faith is to define oneself, thereby entrapping oneself within a role, within a set of behaviors. This can be done in a variety of ways, for example, I may define myself in terms of my occupation, or in terms of my personality type. In the first case, I might believe that because I am, say, a surgeon, I must engage in certain typical surgeon-like behaviors. For instance, I might refrain from heavy drinking before performing surgery, speak in consequential tones during surgery, and play golf after surgery. To do so is not necessarily bad faith, but if I do these things because I believe that I cannot do otherwise, because I *am* a surgeon, and these are surgeon-like behaviors, then I live in bad faith because, in that case, my following what I take to be a surgeon's life is grounded in my defining myself in terms of my occupation, in my belief that my occupation gives me an identity, that it makes me what I am. In Sartrean terms, I allow my ego, which consists of surgeon-like ego-content accrued through surgeon-like activities, to determine the sort of person that I am, to give me an identity, and thus to determine my behavior. And this amounts to a denial of my own freedom insofar as freedom, for Sartre, refers to the fact that ego-content does not set restrictions on one's actions because this content, originating in acts of empty consciousness, is revisable, and so does not give one an identity. In the case under consideration, no amount of accrued surgeon-content determines me to continue acting in a surgeon-like manner. And, according to Sartre, the same analysis holds for all ego-content, whether it is content that is definitive of one's occupation, such as surgeon-content, of one's personality, such as stinginess-content, or of anything else. To allow any ego-content to determine my behavior is to deny my freedom, and thus to live in bad faith.

The human being's lack of identity also underlies Sartre's claim that we are completely responsible for our actions, and for what we make of ourselves. We touched on this point briefly in our section on Sartre's ontology. There, we saw that because all ego-content is produced by acts of empty consciousness, human beings are born without yet possessing any content, or that the human being's existence temporally precedes its essence. And because our own free actions give us whatever content we accrue, we make ourselves into the type of person that we are; we are completely responsible for our own ego. Moreover, the ego-content that we do accrue is revisable, again, by our own free actions. For the human being's existence precedes its essence, not only temporally but also ontologically. That is, ego-content is unilaterally dependent upon acts of free consciousness. Therefore, we continue, throughout our life, to make ourselves into the type of person that we are. We never cease to be completely responsible for every act of our own ego. So, although there may be many influences on my behavior, and thus on my being the type of person that I am, such as the environment in which I was raised, the ultimate responsibility for my actions lies fully on my own shoulders.

Returning, now, to the ethical consequences of Sartre's position, we can see how it leaves the basic problem of an existentialist ethics unresolved. And here lies the aforementioned true radicality of Sartre's position. Because of his claim that the human being completely lacks an identity, he is left with no self to be achieved, and thus without any standard, whether determinate or indeterminate, for judging human self-achievement, that is, without a standard for ethical judgment. Sartre's ontology of the human being's radical indeterminacy forces him to deny ethical judgment altogether—in the final analysis, anything goes.

VI. EXISTENTIALIST ETHICS

At the beginning of this chapter, we noted that the existentialist's rejection of rationalist ontology, and of the exact, unambiguous type of cognition that articulates the objects of rationalist ontology, is undeniably problematic insofar as it jeopardizes our ability to properly classify objects. We also noted that the ethical consequences of existentialist ontology are more problematic still because such an ontology similarly jeopardizes our ability to classify actions as good or evil—it jeopardizes the very enterprise of morality.

We have now seen four paradigm examples of existentialist ethical theories, of ethical theories maintaining that there are no rational, unambiguous principles for ethical judgment, and we have seen how these theories address the problem concerning that which becomes of morality when such principles are rejected. In Nietzsche's case, his ontology of will to power implies that the standard for judging human action is indeterminate. The person who lives in accordance with such a standard, Nietzsche's overman, does not live a life to which ethical judgment is simply inapplicable but, rather, one in which such judgments are uncertain because of the indeterminacy of the standard in terms of which they are effected. Kierkegaard's ontology of individuality also implies an indeterminate standard for judging human action. In his case, the religious person lives in accordance with such a standard, and the religious person, like the Nietzschean overman, does not live a life in which all is permitted, but one in which judgments concerning the propriety of actions are always uncertain. Similarly, Heidegger's ontology of indeterminacy, which is based on the impossibility of our gaining a full understanding of being, implies an indeterminate standard for human action—the standard of authenticity. In all three of the previous cases, the threat of absolute permissiveness that the loss of rational, univocal standards for ethical judgment occasions is dissolved through the introduction of indeterminate standards, along with irrational, ambiguous ways of cognizing them. In Sartre's case, however, this threat, which, as we have seen, is the fundamental problem faced by existentialist ethics, remains unresolved. For Sartre, the human being is completely without identity, and so without a standard for judging its behavior.

To conclude, let us note the negative and positive consequences of existentialist ethics. Previously, we noted that existentialism is reputed to be a pessimistic, destructive philosophy because its rejection of the world's rationality seems to undermine some of Western culture's most basic institutions, such as science and morality. At the end of our chapter on existentialist ontology, we saw that existentialist ontology does entail a rejection of science, though not of all knowledge; it allows for a type of cognition of the world that is geared to the world's true indeterminacy. Thus, an apparently negative consequence of existentialist irrationalism was seen as a positive consequence; that is, for the existentialist, the rejection of science is the rejection of a type of cognition that is based on a falsification of the world's true nature. A similar claim can be made for existentialism's assessment of morality.

By denying the existence of determinate standards for ethical judgment, it certainly seems, at first glance, that existentialism must succumb to an outright rejection of morality as a whole. And although, as we have now seen, this is not necessarily the case, we can, at least, agree that this loss of univocal criteria is a negative consequence of existentialism insofar as it strips our ethical judgments of certainty. That is, even when we recognize that the existentialist's denial of univocal ethical standards still leaves room for indeterminate standards, the uncertainty that judgments according to such indeterminate criteria carry leaves us in a more difficult position for making moral judgments than we would be in if we had determinate criteria at our disposal. However, this apparently negative aspect of existentialist ethics is seen as positive if we accept an existentialist ontology of indeterminacy. That is, if we agree that the world is ambiguous, and that this implies the indeterminacy of ethical standards, then any conception of morality that maintains certainty in our moral judgments is seen as illusory, rather than being seen as preferable to a morality of uncertainty. Just like existentialism's rejection of science, its rejection of a morality based on determinate standards turns out to be a positive consequence of existentialist irrationalism because it leads to the search for a type of life that is in keeping with the true nature of human existence. Even in the case of Sartre's complete rejection of morality, which seems to be an irredeemably negative position insofar as morality disappears altogether, we must admit that if he is right about the impropriety of all ethical judgment, then the entire institution of morality should be rejected.

Ultimately, existentialism gives us a picture of the world and of our place in it that might not be terribly palatable to most of us. The world of the existentialist makes less sense than we might like it to, and the life endorsed by the existentialist is more difficult to negotiate. But this is certainly no reason to reject the existentialist's position. After all, the degree to which a belief makes us comfortable is not a measure of its truth.

Selected Bibliography

PRIMARY SOURCES

1. Martin Heidegger, *Being and Time*, trans. Joan Stambaugh, State University of New York Press, Albany, 1996.

2. Martin Heidegger, *Introduction to Metaphysics*, trans. Gregory Fried and Richard Polt, Yale University Press, New Haven, CT, 2000.

3. Søren Kierkegaard, *Either/Or*, Volume I, trans. David Swenson and Lillian Marvin Swenson, Princeton University Press, Princeton, NJ, 1959.

4. Søren Kierkegaard, *Either/Or*, Volume II, trans. Walter Lowrie, Princeton University Press, Princeton, NJ, 1959.

5. Søren Kierkegaard, *Fear and Trembling; Repetition*, trans. Howard V. Hong and Edna H. Hong, Princeton University Press, Princeton, NJ, 1983.

6. Friedrich Nietzsche, *Beyond Good and Evil*, trans. Walter Kaufman, Vintage Books, New York, 1966.

7. Friedrich Nietzsche, *The Birth of Tragedy* and *The Genealogy of Morals*, trans. Francis Golffing, Anchor Books, New York, 1956.

8. Friedrich Nietzsche, *The Gay Science*, trans. Walter Kaufman, Vintage Books, New York, 1974.

9. Friedrich Nietzsche, *Philosophy in the Tragic Age of the Greeks*, trans. Marianne Cowan, Gateway Editions, Chicago, 1962.

10. Jean-Paul Sartre, *Being and Nothingness*, trans. Hazel Barnes, Pocket Books, New York, 1956.

11. Jean-Paul Sartre, "Existentialism is a Humanism," from *Existentialism from Dostoevsky to Sartre*, ed. Walter Kaufman, World Publishing, New York, 1956.

12. Jean-Paul Sartre, *The Transcendence of the Ego*, trans. Forrest Williams and Robert Kirkpatrick, Hill and Wang, New York, 1960.

RECOMMENDED SECONDARY SOURCES

General

1. William Barrett, *What is Existentialism?*, Random House, New York, 1964.

2. Mary Warnock, *Existentialism*, Oxford University Press, New York, 1970.

3. John Wild, *The Challenge on Existentialism*, Indiana University Press, Bloomington, 1966.

Heidegger

1. Hubert Dreyfus, *Being-in-the-World*, MIT University Press, Cambridge, MA, 1991

2. William Richardson, *Heidegger: Through Phenomenology to Thought*, Martinus Nijhoff, The Hague, 1974.

Kierkegaard

1. Walter Lowrie, *Kierkegaard*, Oxford University Press, New York, 1938.

2. Louis Mackey, *Kierkegaard: A Kind of Poet*, University of Pennsylvania Press, Philadelphia, 1971.

Nietzsche

1. Arthur Danto, *Nietzsche as Philosopher*, Macmillan, New York, 1965.

2. Richard Schacht, *Nietzsche*, Routledge and Kegan Paul, London, 1983.

Sartre

1. Hazel Barnes, *Sartre*, Lippincott, New York, 1973.

2. Peter Caws, *Sartre*, Routledge and Kegan Paul, London, 1979.